JESUS
OF NAZARETH

JESUS
OF NAZARETH

William Barclay

Based on the film directed by Franco Zeffirelli
from the script by Anthony Burgess, Suso Cecchi d'Amico
and Franco Zeffirelli

Collins
FOUNTAIN BOOKS

First published in Fountain Books 1977
© RAI   I.T.C. Entertainment Limited
and William Barclay, 1977

Made and printed in Great Britain by
William Collins Sons & Co. Ltd, Glasgow

Contents

Introduction

This book is based on Anthony Burgess' script of the television film of *Jesus of Nazareth*. The script of the film was in my hands when I wrote it, and there are large areas of the book where I did no more than change the script into narrative form.

It may well be that there are some who think it is an irreverence to make the life of Jesus into a film, but there are fewer and fewer people who read and more and more who learn by looking at pictures. I therefore regard the writing of this book as an opportunity to be seized.

Every generation has its own method of learning. For long, the method of learning in the English-speaking countries has been by way of the book and the written word. More and more this has been changing until the method of learning has been through the picture. This book will bring the life of Jesus into the lives of many, which could not have been brought in in any other way. The eye-gate to learning has always been stronger than the ear-gate, and this book has been designed to appeal to the eye-gate through the remarkable film stills which accompany the text.

In the film and in this book the story of Jesus is told simply and straightforwardly. There is no attempt at sensationalism. The story, in all its simplicity, is allowed to make its own impact. It may well be that the seeing of this film may send viewers back to the gospels themselves, and if they do go back to the gospels, they will read them with a new intelligence and a new vividness after seeing this film. It is our hope that this book may enable ordinary people to see Jesus more vividly and may move them to commit their lives to him.

William Barclay

PART I

The Coming

Although only a small town in a tiny province Nazareth was far from being remote. Traffic from the ends of the earth passed close to its borders. A boy had only to climb the hill at the back of the town to see the Road of the Sea which came up from Egypt and went out to Damascus, along which the great trading caravans with their strings of laden camels moved constantly. He would see also the Road of the East running from the Mediterranean to Parthia and beyond, along which trading adventurers passed to remote lands, and the Roman legions clanked their way to service on the eastern frontiers of the Empire. He had only to look westward and the blue waters of the Mediterranean lay shimmering before him, dotted with ships sailing to Egypt, to Greece and to Rome. An imaginative boy brought up in Nazareth could not fail to have dreams and visions which reached out to the ends of the earth.

While its situation encouraged the youth of Nazareth to dream of far-away places, political conditions excited their elders, like Jews everywhere, to dream of the future – of a Golden Age when all the world would bow to the coming Jewish Messiah. The dreams varied strangely, however. Some were of a worldwide Empire under a conquering Messiah who would impose his will by force. Others were of a universal rule founded on love and truth, to which all would freely and joyfully assent. And while many dreamed, there were some who plotted direct action here and now to cast off the Roman yoke.

Discussions about the future went on everywhere including the house of Yehuda the Rabbi. There were sceptics, like Jotham, who had lost faith in messianic dreams. The prophets had long been dead, and their unfulfilled predictions had become mere irrelevances. But a future without hope, said the Rabbi, was like a night without stars; and he reminded them of the signs that would herald the dawn of the new age, 'then the eyes of the blind shall be opened, and the ears of the deaf unstopped; then shall the lame man leap as an hart, and the tongue of the dumb sing for joy', and there was that greatest sign of all: 'A virgin shall conceive and bear a son'.

Herod the Great ruled in Palestine when Jesus was born. In many ways a great king he was driven almost mad by fear of treachery from those close to the throne, and his insane suspicions of his nearest and dearest impelled him to murder his wife Amariamme, her mother Alexandra, his sons Alexander, Aristobulus and Antipater. As Augustus the Roman Emperor, making a play on the Greek words, cynically remarked, it was safer to be Herod's *hus* (pig) than to be his *huios* (son).

Herod ruled by permission of Rome and as a consequence was hated by the Jews, who despised him also since he was half Idumaean. He tried, unsuccessfully, to win popular favour by a lavish rebuilding of the Jewish temple. But he would tolerate no intrusion of religion into politics, and any man with claims to being a prophet was closely watched. So long as his message was innocuously non-political he was left alone, but if the righteousness he proclaimed acquired a political connotation he was effectively silenced, if necessary by being killed. Anyone with the remotest claim to being Messiah was eliminated at once, for the last thing Herod wanted was a rebellion against Rome, which would immediately cost him his throne.

There was a devout family living in Nazareth during Herod's reign, the head of which, Joachin, died, leaving Anna his widow with only a daughter, Mary, who was engaged to marry Joseph, the village carpenter. As a carpenter Joseph was a craftsman of some standing, and he came of a distinguished family, for he was a direct descendant of King David.

Then to Mary's astonishment and no small dread, the angel Gabriel appeared to her, bringing a message from God. 'Joy be with you!' he said. 'You are specially dear to God! The Lord is with you!' She was deeply moved at what he said, and wondered what a greeting like this could mean. 'Don't be afraid, Mary,' the angel said to her, 'God has chosen you for a very precious privilege. You will conceive, and you will have a son, and you must give him the name Jesus. He will be great; his title will be "the Son of the Most High". The Lord will give him the throne of David his ancestor. He will reign over the house of Jacob for ever, and his reign will never come to an end.' Mary said to the angel, 'How can this happen when I have no husband?' The angel answered, 'The Holy Spirit will come upon you, and the power of the Most High will overshadow you. That is why the holy child who will be born will be called Son of God. Elisabeth, your kinswoman, has also conceived a son in her old age. They said that she could never have a child. But now she is in her sixth month, for there is nothing impossible to God.' Mary said, 'I am the Lord's servant. Whatever you say, I accept.' And the angel went away and left her.

In this way Mary learnt that she was to have a child without human paternity, who would be the Messiah.

She had already heard the remarkable news of her kinswoman, Elisabeth, who was pregnant although long past the age of child-bearing; and she at once decided to set out for the small Judean town where Elisabeth lived and visit her. When she arrived the baby stirred in Elisabeth's womb, and Elisabeth burst into inspired speech:

'You are the most blessed of women and blessed is the child you will bear. Why have I received this privilege that the mother of my Lord should come to me? For, when I heard your greeting, the baby in my womb leaped for joy. Blessed is she who has believed that the message she received from the Lord will come true.'

And Mary answered:

'My soul tells me of the greatness of God,
    and my spirit thrills in God my Saviour,
    because he has looked kindly on his servant,
    even though my place in life is humble.
From now on those of all time to come will call me
    blessed, for the mighty One has done great things for
    me, and holy is his name.
His mercy is from age to age
    to those who reverence him
He has done mighty deeds with his right arm.
He has scattered the proud with their arrogant plans.
He has thrown down the mighty from their seats of
    power.
He has exalted the humble.
He has filled those who are hungry with good things,
    and those who are rich he has sent empty away.
He has come to the aid of Israel his servant.
He has kept the promise that he made to our fathers,
    the promise never to forget his mercy to Abraham,
    and to his descendants for ever.'

Mary stayed with Elisabeth for three months and then
returned home. Her personal problem was then inescapable.
She had to tell her mother and Joseph that she was carrying
a child which had been conceived without intercourse.
Joseph, unable to credit her story, was heartbroken. He
consulted with the village rabbi, who could do no better
than quote the law to him, which left him no option but to
annul the marriage contract. He was anxious not to shame
Mary publicly, however, and planned to divorce her in
secret. At this pass he too received a message from God. It
reached him through a dream in which the angel of the Lord
appeared and spoke to him.

'Joseph, son of David,' the angel said, 'do not hesitate to
marry Mary, for it is as a result of the action of the Holy
Spirit that she is going to have a child. She will have a son,
and you must call him by the name Jesus, for it is he who
will save his people from their sins.' All this happened that

the statement made by the Lord through the prophet might come true:

'The virgin shall conceive and have a child,
and they shall give him the name Emmanuel'

for that name means 'God is with us'. So Joseph woke from sleep and carried out the instructions of the angel of the Lord. He married Mary and she had her son and they called him by the name Jesus.

So Joseph believed that Mary had spoken the truth, and they were married.

As the time for the child's birth drew near, Rome decreed that a census of the whole Empire must be taken. The decree was highly unpopular, for it was common knowledge that censuses were taken to determine the number of men liable for military service, and to bring the registers relating to taxation up to date.

To the Jews a census was particularly obnoxious, for their religious traditions were against it, and a census imposed by a foreign power mocked their most sacred principle: 'No rule but the Lord, no King but God.' To prevent violent outbursts while the census was being taken, the Romans therefore ordered each man to be registered, not at his place of residence, but at the headquarters of his clan or tribe. In this way dangerous combinations of the rebellious might be avoided, for while a man could trust the friends and neighbours of his home town, he would be cautious about plotting with strangers.

The conditions of the census thus forced Joseph to travel from his home in Nazareth to Bethlehem, the ancestral town of David, to whose family he belonged. Mary would have to travel with him, and when they were due to depart the time for Mary's delivery would be so near that her child was virtually certain to be born in Bethlehem. Realizing this Joseph was astonished and deeply moved, for he remembered the prophecy of Micah: 'But thou, O Bethlehem, from you shall come forth for me one who is to be ruler of Israel.' Thus by reason of the census Mary's baby would be delivered in the very town which prophecy identified as the birthplace of the Messiah. Any last lingering doubts Joseph retained about Mary's astonishing story were swept away, and he wholly and joyfully believed.

For Mary the long journey to Bethlehem was exhausting, and they arrived to find the inns so crowded that Joseph could secure no accommodation for her. But at one place where they were turned away, a serving girl, distressed by Mary's condition, told them of a stable where they could find shelter. It would at least be warm and dry. Mary's need was then so acute that they gratefully accepted the girl's suggestion, and it was in a stable that Mary was delivered and Jesus was born.

It was not long before the newly-born infant had his first visitors. During the night hours some shepherds were in the fields outside Bethlehem keeping watch over their sheep. The guard was needed against human as much as animal predators, for the great influx of visitors to Bethlehem had raised food prices and increased the value of sheep. The shepherds were doubtless themselves hoping to sell their lambs at a very high price. They were rough men, but like peasants everywhere they were shrewd. It was to these men that God's messenger Gabriel also appeared. Thus Luke tells the story:

'In that district there were shepherds out in the fields, guarding their flock by night. An angel of the Lord appeared to them, and the glory of the Lord shone round them, and they were terrified. "Don't be afraid," the angel said to them, "for I am bringing you good news of great joy, a joy in which all peoples will share. For today there has been born to you in David's town a saviour who is the Messiah, the Lord. This is how you will recognize him. You will find a baby, wrapped in swaddling clothes, lying in a manger." Suddenly there was with the angel a crowd of heaven's army, singing God's praise. "Glory to God in the heights of heaven," they sang, "and on earth peace to mankind, on whom God's favour rests".'

14

When the angels had left them and returned to heaven, the shepherds exclaimed, 'What wonders of God are these!' And one said, 'Come! we must risk leaving the sheep. At all costs we must go to Bethlehem and see the child the angels have told us about.' So they hurried to the town as fast as their legs would carry them. There they found Mary and Joseph with the baby lying in the manger, as the angels had said.

When they came away they could not contain themselves, but told everyone they met of their wonderful experience. Those who heard of it were astonished and told others, and so the story was spread about. The shepherds then went back to their sheep glorifying and praising God for all that they had heard and seen. And Mary treasured the memory of their coming, wondering at all that was happening.

The shepherds were not the only visitors to the stable. Others, strangely different, were coming a long way to find him. Caspar, Melchior and Balthasar were magi from the East, men of great learning who studied the night sky in their own separate countries, believing they could read in the stars predictions of future events on earth. In the year Jesus was born the planets Jupiter and Saturn met in the sign of the zodiac called Pisces, the Fish. The conjunction takes place only once every 794 years, and it is a brilliant sight. The magi held Pisces to be the sign of *the last days*; Jupiter they regarded as the star of *the world ruler*; while Saturn was *the star of Palestine*. They therefore reckoned that when Jupiter met Saturn in the constellation of Pisces, the ruler of the last days would appear in Palestine; and they travelled to Palestine to find him, bringing him gifts.

Before they could find Jesus the story of their coming reached Herod. When he learnt that they had come to find a new king his suspicious fears were at once aroused, and he intended to murder the child who would, as he thought, be a threat to his own power.

In due time the baby Jesus was brought to the synagogue to be circumcised. There was present in the synagogue an aged saint named Simeon, who 'meticulously observed the Law and devoutly reverenced God,' as St Luke say , and who had become assured through the Holy Spirit 'that death would not come to him until he had seen the Lord's Messiah'. When he saw Jesus he took him in his arms and said:

'Now, O Lord, as you promised,
you are giving your servant his release in peace,
because my eyes have seen the saving power
which you have prepared for all peoples to see,
to be a light to bring your revelation to the Gentiles,
and glory to your people Israel.'

Mary and Joseph returned with Jesus to the stable and there found the three magi waiting for them with their gifts of gold, frankincense and myrrh.

The magi, who had learnt about Herod's real purpose, warned Mary and Joseph to leave Palestine and they accordingly took the baby Jesus and set out on the long road to Egypt. The magi, to evade Herod, meanwhile returned to their own land by another route. When he realized that he had been tricked Herod's rage knew no bounds, and he ordered the slaughter of every male child in Bethlehem up to the age of two.

PART 2

Preparing the Way

In due time Herod the Great died, and his death presented the Romans with a problem. Whatever the Jews thought about him, from the standpoint of Rome Herod was an eminently satisfactory ruler, who had succeeded in keeping Palestine quiet and trouble free. None of his sons had inherited his ability as a ruler, however, and Augustus decided to split Palestine between the three of them. Judea was entrusted to Archelaus despite the fact that he was so unpopular with the Jews that they sent an Embassy to Rome requesting that he should not become their ruler; Philip, the best of the sons, was given Ituraea. Galilee was handed over to Herod Antipas, whom Jesus was to call 'that fox'.

In due time news of Herod's death and the redistribution of his Kingdom reached Egypt. When Joseph heard about it he immediately made preparations to return home, although he was warned to avoid Jerusalem which was wracked with troubles under the unsatisfactory Archelaus.

Joseph and Mary thus returned to Palestine. Anna was dead, but there were many to give them an astonished welcome, having never thought to see them again. They took over Anna's house and Joseph got the carpenter's shop going again. Meanwhile Archelaus had made such a mess of things in Judea that the Romans finally exiled him, and replaced him with a Roman procurator whose headquarters were in Caesarea on the sea coast.

Even in Nazareth the new political set-up made itself felt. There was, for instance, the day when a squadron of Roman cavalry, on its way from Damascus to Jerusalem, appeared in the village and proceeded to seize everything eatable. Reminded that Nazareth was in Galilee, and Galilee was not under direct Roman rule, they answered that an army on the road must eat, and added proudly that as far as they were concerned the whole world was Rome.

Such conduct gave great offence to all, but it enraged the Zealots, a party whose name signified their zeal for the Jewish law. So fanatical were they that when a law was broken they were prepared to murder the offender, be he Jew or Gentile. Believing the Jews should acknowledge no king but God, they longed and schemed for the day when they would be strong enough to make a successful armed rebellion against the hated Romans.

Always on the verge of revolt, seeking all the time for a leader who could carry them to victory, when an incident like the soldiers' raid on Nazareth occurred the younger Zealots in particular were hard to control.

Meanwhile the boy Jesus was growing up. He played in the carpenter's shop and would sometimes climb a ladder Joseph was making to see the roads going north, south and east, and glimpse the sparkle of the blue waters of the Mediterranean away to the west: and dreams of a world would fill his mind.

He attended the village school where Rabbi Yehuda taught. One day the Rabbi was giving the class a test in unseen reading. He handed a scroll to the boys one after another, but they could make nothing of it. Then came the turn of Jesus. Clearly and easily Jesus read:

The Lord is my shepherd. He leadeth me to green pastures, and maketh me to lie by the quiet waters.

The Rabbi was deeply impressed by the boy's progress. 'And do you know who wrote it?' he asked. 'My great, great, great, great, great, great grandfather, King David,' he answered. Jesus knew his ancestry even as a boy.

The day came when he officially 'grew up'. In Palestine, a boy became a man on his twelfth birthday. From that time onwards he was personally responsible for keeping the law: he was eligible to be a witness in a law-court; he could take part in the reading of the Scripture Lesson and the discussion in the synagogue. A ceremony initiating the boy into becoming *Bar Mitzwah*, a son of the law, was held in the synagogue. It continues among the Jews to this day, and part of the prayer which the boy prays is as follows:

O my God and God of my fathers, on this solemn and sacred day, which marks my passage from boyhood to manhood, I humbly raise my eyes unto thee, and declare with sincerity and truth, that henceforth I will keep thy commandments, and undertake and bear the responsibility of my actions towards thee. In my earliest infancy I was brought within thy sacred covenant with Israel: and today I again enter, as an active responsible member, into this elect congregation, in the midst of which I will never cease to proclaim thy holy name in the face of all nations.

Doubtless Jesus used the prayer on the day he became a *Bar Mitzwah* in the synagogue in Nazareth.

Having become officially an adult, Jesus had to fulfil certain religious duties. Every adult male Jew was obliged to attend three annual festivals at Jerusalem: Passover, Pentecost and Tabernacles. Greatest of all was the Passover, for which the most careful preparation had to be made. For six weeks, as the time for it approached, it was the subject of sermons in the synagogue and lessons in school. Like other Jewish boys, Jesus prepared to attend his first Passover.

Jerusalem was a hundred miles from Nazareth, and the caravan from the village, slow-moving for the sake of mothers and children, took about a week on the journey.

What a thrill it was when the Temple came in sight! Josephus describes its dazzling appearance. 'The outward face of the Temple in its front wanted nothing that was likely either to surprise men's minds or their eyes; for it was covered all over with plates of gold of great weight and, at the first rising of the sun reflected back a very fiery splendour and made those who forced themselves to look upon it to turn away their eyes, just as they would at the sun's own rays. The Temple appeared to strangers when they were at a distance like the mountain covered with snow, for those parts of it which were not gilt were exceedingly white.' As they marched on their way, and especially as they were climbing Mount Sion to the sacred city, the pilgrims sang what the English Bible calls 'The Songs of Ascents', Psalms 120–134. 'I was glad when they said to me, "Let us go into the house of the Lord".'

What would Jesus see when he came into Jerusalem for the first time? As he came to the city gates he would see both sides of the road lined with scaffolds for those who were to be executed. Next, the Temple. He would be instructed beforehand as to its layout, but it was built in a series of courts. The outermost was the Court of the Gentiles, into which anyone might come but beyond which no Gentile must pass. Next was the Court of the Women, into which all Jews could enter but beyond which no woman must go. Then came the Court of the Israelites, beyond which no layman must venture. Finally there was the Court of the Priests, with the great altar and, at the far end, the Holy Place and the Holy of Holies, which no one might enter except the High Priest, and he only once a year on the Day of Atonement.

The Court of the Gentiles presented an extraordinary spectacle. In it the merchants who sold pigeons and lambs for the sacrifices had their shops, and the money-changers had their tables. The place was like a busy market rather than part of the Temple.

The main part of the Passover Meal was the lamb. It commemorated the deliverance from Egypt, when a last terrible plague broke Pharaoh's resistance and he allowed the Israelites to depart. An angel of death was to pass through the land and slay the first-born son in every Egyptian household. To keep their own homes unscathed the Israelites were instructed to mark the lintel of their doorposts with the blood of a lamb, and the avenging angel would *pass over* the houses so marked. The Passover Feast was eaten in the evening in the homes of the people, but before that, the lamb which was the main part of the feast, had first to be offered in the Temple. The blood of the animal was sacred to God, for the Jews identified the blood with the life. The lamb had therefore to be slaughtered by a priest and its blood poured on to the altar. Something of what the Temple courts must have been like can be gauged from the fact that a census of lambs slain at the Passover of year 65, when Cestius Gallus was governor, established a figure of 256,500 animals sacrificed in that one year alone. It baffles the imagination to think what the altar must have been like after the blood of more than a quarter of a million lambs had been poured on it. The number of lambs gives us an idea of the number of people in Jerusalem at Passover time. A Passover house gathering had to consist of a minimum of ten people to each lamb. This means that well over 2,565,000 were packed into Jerusalem at Passover time.

It was Jesus who was holding in his arms the lamb which the group from Nazareth wished sacrificed. He handed over the lamb with a look of intense sorrow in his eyes. In his heart he seemed to be sharing the tragedy of the lamb, while a Levite's voice was repeating Isaiah's famous words:

He was despised and rejected of men; a man of sorrows and acquainted with grief; and we hid as it were our faces from him; he was despised and we esteemed him not. Surely he has borne our griefs and carried our sorrow; yet we did esteem him stricken, smitten of God, and afflicted.

All we like sheep have gone astray; we have turned every one to his own way; and the Lord has laid on him the iniquity of us all. He was oppressed and he was afflicted, yet he opened not his mouth; he is brought as a lamb to the slaughter, and as a sheep before her shearers is dumb so he openeth not his mouth.

He was wounded for our transgressions, he was bruised for our iniquities; the chastisement of our peace was upon him; and with his stripes we are healed.

When the lamb was handed back to be the Passover Meal, its body was slit down the middle and kept open by two pieces of wood – in the form of a cross.

The lamb slain, the cross of wood, the words from Isaiah – hints of his destiny were beginning to enter the mind of the boy Jesus.

So the ancient ritual unfolded. It was partly memory of the past:

O Lord, thou hast given us this day of the Passover that we may re-live our exodus. Glory to thee, O Lord, who blessest Israel and the feasts thereof.

It was partly hope for the future.

This is the bread of affliction that our fathers ate in the land of Egypt. He who hungers, let him come and eat with us. This night we are in bondage; tomorrow we shall be free.

In this way they remembered the day when God had delivered them from bondage in Egypt, and hoped for the day when God would deliver them from bondage to Rome.

The time came for Joseph and Mary to set out with the caravan on the return to Nazareth. The women left first because they walked more slowly. The men followed later. The men caught up and they were all together at the evening halting place. It was then that Mary and Joseph discovered that Jesus was not with them. Up to that time neither had worried, because Mary had thought that he was with Joseph and Joseph supposed that he was with his mother. They hurried to the caravan master who told them that he must be with the other children in the centre of the caravan; but Jesus was not there. There was nothing for it, they must go back to Jerusalem and look for him.

What had Jesus been doing in his time alone in Jerusalem? He had seen the women of the streets flirt with the Roman soldiers. He had seen criminals being led to the place of execution, carrying the cross-piece of the gibbets to which they would be nailed. As he watched, someone in the crowd quoted scripture: 'Cursed be he who hangs from the wood of the tree'.

With sinking hearts Joseph and Mary searched all through the streets of Jerusalem, but they could not find him. At last they turned their footsteps to the Temple. The Sanhedrin, the supreme court of Jews which settled all points of faith and doctrine, ethics and law, was in session. Normally it met in private but during Passover time it met publicly in the Temple colonnades. Its arguments and discussions for this one week were open to all. And it was there that Joseph and Mary found Jesus, young as he was, listening to the members of the Sanhedrin, speaking and asking them questions, taking a full part in the discussions. Mary went to Jesus. 'Son,' she said, 'why did you do this to us? Your father and I have been searching everywhere for you, and we have been desperately worried.'

'Did you not know,' said Jesus, 'that I must be in my Father's house?'

When Jesus was thirty years old, John the Baptist suddenly emerged on the national scene. John was a child of the desert. He had gone into the wilderness, far from cities and their thronging crowds, and in rugged solitude had lived close to nature, near to God. Suddenly he issued a prophetic call, startling in its passion and conviction, for a return to righteousness. People streamed out to the place by the Jordan where he preached, and hundreds responded to his call and were baptized in the river in token of repentance from their sins.

National groups reacted to him in differing ways. While the Zealots saw him as a potential rabble-rouser, and wanted to use him for their cause, the Pharisees resented his searing call to repentance. Were they not sons of Abraham? And did not descent from Abraham guarantee salvation? They even had a saying that God had stationed an angel at the mouth of hell to turn back any descendant of Abraham who mistakenly arrived there. John told them that God could, if he chose, turn the very stones of the desert into sons of Abraham. What mattered was not a man's ancestry but his own living, the way he treated his fellow men.

The Sadducees, who had control of the priesthood and the Temple, were incensed by an unofficial religious movement. They sent to ask John who he thought he was and where he got his authority. John answered that his authority was from God, and that he was a forerunner of one whose very sandal he was not worthy to untie, and who would baptize them not with water but with the Holy Spirit and with fire.

By this time Joseph had died. He was sad to leave Mary, for he knew that Jesus would not remain with her much longer. 'We have always known,' he said, 'that it was not for us that he came to earth.' So he died, whispering with his last breath, as Jesus was also one day to do, 'Into thy hands I commend my spirit'.

News of John's crusade was the signal for Jesus to leave home. He went with the crowds to hear John preach, and presented himself for baptism in the river. John had a sudden flash of recognition and said, 'It is I who should be baptized by you, and yet you come to me'. Jesus raised him up. 'Let it be so,' he said, 'it is only right for us to do everything a good man ought to do.' John then consented to baptize Jesus, and there came a voice from heaven: 'This is my son, the beloved, the only one, in whom I am well pleased.'

With his baptism something momentous happened to Jesus. He knew that for him the hour had struck. He must begin the work for which he had come into the world. But how was he to proceed? He had to gain the attention of men and then to win their allegiance. There were alternative methods he could use, and it would be fatally easy to choose the wrong way. He therefore went out into the wilderness to reflect over the alternatives, and reject alluring short-cuts. As the gospels put it, he went into the desert to be tempted of the Devil. We must not think of the conflict happening, as it were, visibly. The whole struggle went on in the mind of Jesus. Nor must we think of the temptations proceeding in three distinct acts. The struggle was being waged in the mind of Jesus all the forty days he was in the wilderness.

The first temptation arose when he was feeling tired and hungry and very much alone. Stones looking like small loaves covered the ground. Conscious of his superhuman power, Jesus felt an impulse to turn the stones into bread. 'Use your powers for your own comfort and security,' the Tempter was inwardly saying to him. But Jesus refused. 'It takes more than bread to keep a man alive,' he answered, 'man lives by every word that comes out of the mouth of God.'

The second temptation was more subtle. 'Look,' whispered the Tempter, 'how can you expect anyone to believe in you? You, an unknown carpenter from Nazareth! Startle them into paying attention. Get God to work a spectacular miracle for you. Jump off the highest spire of the Temple and float down and land unharmed. That will impress the people and they will assuredly follow you.' But Jesus refused to use the power of God for magical displays. 'You must never try,' he said, 'to see how far you can go with God and get away with it.'

In the third temptation the inner voice said, 'Think of the poor, the enslaved, the deprived, the suffering. They wait for your coming and desperately need your help. You will be unable to tackle a problem so vast and bring them relief, unless you have *power*. Follow my way and I will give you mastery over the whole earth.' Here the temptation was to compromise, to seek first the visible power and glory of this world. But again Jesus refused. He had come not to be served but to serve, and he must serve God alone if he was to bring to men the help they so desperately needed.

Thus Jesus conquered the Tempter, and when day broke and morning came he left the desert, his mind made up, and returned to mingle again with men.

PART 3

Fisher of Men

Very soon after he had emerged from his temptation experience, Jesus returned to Nazareth. Two women who saw him come into the town raced to tell Mary that he was back and that he had gone straight to the synagogue. So Mary prepared herself and also went down to the synagogue. It was the Sabbath and the congregation was just finishing the recital of the 18 Benedictions. The Rabbi had read from the Law and it was now time for the lesson from the Prophets. It was the custom for someone from the congregation to read the lesson from the Prophets and the Rabbi looked round to see who could best be called. Before he had made up his mind, however, Jesus came forward and taking up the roll began to read. He read from the book of the prophet Isaiah:

> The spirit of the Lord is upon me
> because he has anointed me to bring good news to the poor.
> He has sent me to announce to the prisoners
> that they will be liberated
> and to the blind that they will see again;
> to send away in freedom those who have been broken by life;
> to announce that the year
> when the favour of God will be shown has come.

Jesus handed back the roll and said quietly, 'Today this passage of scripture has come true as you listened to it.' At first there was a shocked silence and then the congregation began to buzz with discontent. One cried out, 'Isn't it

Joseph's son, the carpenter?' Another, 'How can he dare to make such a claim!' Yet a third, 'What do you mean? The prophecy you read can be fulfilled only by the Messiah, at the coming of the Kingdom of God.' There were murmurs of indignant agreement from the scandalized congregation. Jesus said, 'The Kingdom of God comes not in a way foreseen by men. The Kingdom of Heaven – behold – is suddenly amongst you. Repent and believe the good news.'

Andrew and Philip, two disciples of John who had followed Jesus to Nazareth, were in the congregation and in Jesus's claim they found the fulfilment of what John had said about him.

While some members of the congregation left the synagogue in high dudgeon, others remained still arguing. Jesus rose to his feet and Yehuda the Rabbi came over to him. Yehuda would have liked to believe in him but found it impossible. He was obviously sorry. Jesus put a hand on his arm and said, 'No prophet is accepted in his own country', and then, in a louder voice, to the entire congregation he said, 'Blessed is he who is not ashamed of me.'

The voices had now become threatening.

'What are we waiting for?'

'Rabbi, make him leave!'

'Cheat!'

'Liar!'

'Twister of the sacred scriptures!'

'How can he be the Messiah, dressed in rags like that?'

'He didn't say he was the Messiah.'

'What else could he mean?'

'Throw him out!'

The women were looking with disapproval at Mary and one said to her, 'Thank God Joseph, your husband, didn't live to see this day.' But Mary was immersed in her own thoughts.

In the roadway outside the synagogue the men of the village had resolved to make an example of Jesus. 'Leave this to us, Rabbi,' said one voice, while another voice cried, 'Throw him over the cliff!' And so when Jesus appeared, in spite of the efforts of some to stop them, they began to hustle him to the cliff outside the town. When they came in sight of the cliff, however, the crowd seemed somehow less determined. Jesus offered no resistance whatever. He and the mob confronted each other. Quite suddenly and quite quietly, the crowd opened up in silence on either side to let him pass through, and Jesus walked serenely away.

As he was walking along the road, Andrew and Philip caught up with him. Andrew said, 'Master, we were sent by John the Prophet to make ourselves known to you. I am Andrew, a fisherman of Capernaum, and this is Philip.'

Jesus answered, 'I am going to Capernaum. Follow me'. And Philip said: 'Gladly'.

'Where is John?' Jesus asked.

'He has been arrested by King Herod Antipas', Philip answered.

As they walked through the fields, Philip said to Jesus, 'John said to us when he saw you, "Behold the Lamb of God. It is Jesus, not me, that you must follow". He also said that anew his joy was fulfilled, and then the soldiers came and took him away.'

They were now in sight of Capernaum. Andrew said to Jesus, 'Anything that attracts crowds is dangerous these days. We saw that again in Nazareth, but,' he went on, 'Capernaum should be a safer place to work from', and he pointed at the town across the lake.

Andrew said, 'It is a bigger town, for one thing. It is less narrow-minded, and I know from experience that the fishermen are ready for a change.' So they came to Capernaum which is a port and one of the largest towns surrounding the lake. It was a frontier town also, through which the road to Damascus and the far east passed. It was therefore an important commercial town, as well as an important fishing port.

Jesus was preaching to a lively congregation in a colonnade at Capernaum. Amongst the listeners there was a young man, John, the John who was one day to write a gospel. He was listening, and smiling sometimes in admiration of Jesus. Jesus said, 'I bring you the good news that you have all awaited. God today fulfils the promise he made to our people Israel, and reconciles himself to you. He reconciles himself to those who are near, and gives peace to those who are far away.' There was a stir among the listeners when Jesus went on, 'Whoever believes in this word will be freed by God from captivity, the captivity of sin. Sin has brought you no satisfaction. You have sold your souls for nothing. And freely God forgives you. He invites you to partake of his banquet. Come, every one of you, sinners and wretches, I proclaim to you the day of forgiveness.'

Thereupon, someone broke in, 'But surely the rewards will be greater for the righteous. Surely people who have observed the Law all their lives will get better places at the banquet than sinners.'

Another man objected, 'Of course God is merciful and can forgive everything, but the sinner must show he is truly repentant and do penance. Do you now suggest that God wants nothing from us in exchange for his forgiveness? Is that right, or have I misunderstood?'

Jesus answered, 'The distance between man and God is vast. No human steps could ever cross it. Here then is the good news I bring to you. You don't have to cross it. God is coming to you to save you, all of you, even the most wretched. Do not shut the door in his face.'

In addition to preaching Jesus performed many striking and merciful acts in Capernaum.

A boy, demon-possessed, violently interrupted him by shouting, 'Leave us alone! What have we to do with you, Jesus of Nazareth? Are you come to torment us? To destroy us?' And the boy fell to the floor, writhing and foaming at the mouth. His father tried, without avail, to help him.

Jesus said to the father, 'How long has he been this way?'

The father answered, 'Since he was a child, and the demon often has thrown him into the fire and into water to destroy him. If you can do anything, have mercy and help us.'

Jesus answered, 'If I can? Everything is possible to him who believes.'

The man answered desperately, 'I believe. Help my poor faith.'

Jesus went over to the boy and addressed him with an imperious gesture. 'Be silent, Satan,' he said, 'I command you unclean spirits from the pit of hell – leave him. Leave him!' The boy went into terrible convulsions and, after a rending paroxysm, he lay still, breathing deeply.

'Take him home,' said Jesus. 'Go in peace.'

This amazing miracle greatly disturbed the congregations. They talked about it to each other and related what had happened to newcomers just arriving.

One old Pharisee addressed Jesus. 'I suspect a danger in all this,' he said. 'Just because you have a certain power – and we admit that, for we saw it exercised just now – we cannot be expected to believe blindly in all that you say. This kind of power doesn't prove anything at all. For all we know it could have come from Satan.'

Jesus smiled at him. 'How can Satan cast out Satan?' he asked. 'If a kingdom is divided against itself, it is bound to collapse. Therefore, it is through God that I cast out devils, and I did it so that you might know that the Kingdom of God has come upon you.'

Jesus and his little group of disciples were walking by the lakeside. There were Andrew and Philip and young John. 'Everyone in our family,' said John, 'is a fisherman. Andrew knows us well. But I was sent off to get learning.'

'All you were fit for perhaps,' said Andrew jestingly.

'And what did you learn?' Jesus asked.

John replied, 'That two and two make four – sometimes. That most people seem to be here to be knocked down. That getting on is a fine thing. That birth is the beginning of death.' John looked intensely at Jesus. 'I have learned,' he said, 'that there is only one Law. The Sadducees now proclaim only the written Law. The Pharisees proclaim the written Law plus all kinds of rules that tradition has added.

We need clarity.'

Jesus put his hand on John's shoulder, and John said, 'Can I stay with you, Rabbi?'

Then they heard voices in the distance, and looking across the lake they saw the silhouettes of the returning fishing boats against a fiery sky. Andrew pointed them out to Jesus. 'There is my brother now, Simon Peter,' and John added, 'And my brother James.'

Peter was shouting in anger as usual, and Andrew said, 'He doesn't really mean it. He is a good man, in spite of his loud mouth.' And Andrew shouted to the boat, 'What's the matter, brother – a poor catch?'

Peter looked up and saw the group on the shore. 'Bad? Bad and bad again. Nothing. Empty nets. Then when I get home the tax-collector buzzes round me like a stinking horsefly. "Where are your taxes?" Well, let him go and catch them. Let him put some fish in the lake.'

Andrew was embarrassed by Peter's roughness, and decided to introduce Jesus to him in the hope that the introduction would take the edge off his anger. Andrew said, 'Peter, this is the man I told you about.'

The boat had reached the shore. Peter stared at the newcomers with suspicion. Jesus walked into the water and placed his hand on the boat, looking at Peter. He said, 'Don't stow your sails. Go out again. I will come with you.'

Peter objected, 'But we've just come in. Pull the boat up!' he ordered his crew.

Andrew went to the boat and implored Peter. 'Peter,' he said, 'please do as Jesus tells you.'

Peter was about to give him a rough answer, but his rage was calming. He was curious to see what the newcomer, Jesus, could do. He looked at Jesus, who was staring out over the lake, indifferent to the dispute between the brothers. Jesus got into the boat and as it began cutting through the waves again, sat in the prow. He leant forward to gaze into the water in which he trailed his hand. Peter and Andrew sat near him. The other boat, carrying James and John, followed closely. Philip was in Peter's boat. Jesus continued leaning over the prow with his eye fixed on the water. Suddenly there was a ruffling of the surface, as if a slight breeze had blown upon it. Jesus cried, 'Now let down your nets!'

Peter made one last objection. 'What do you mean,' he said, 'I tell you there are no fish. I've been fishing for hours without result.' But he obeyed all the same, as did the others. The nets were lowered between the two boats and the ropes tightened. The fishermen shouted excitedly, 'Pull! Pull! Pull!' The nets were pulled to the surface, crammed with fish. Peter pulled with all his might. Although he was bent with the effort, he turned his face towards Jesus: 'Who are you? What are you?' he cried, amazed. Jesus answered, 'You must follow me, and I will make you fishers of men.'

When they regained the shore the lakeside was crowded with people. Other fishermen hurried over to discuss the record catch. Women and children came running to see the great sight of the overladen boats. Even Malachi and Nahum, two Pharisees who worked as basket weavers, had left their work to see what was happening.

The town square of Capernaum was the wealthiest part of the town. There merchants offered their finest wares for sale, there money-changers set up their stalls, and there the

1. To Mary's astonishment the angel Gabriel appeared to her, bringing a message from God
2. It was in a stable that Mary was delivered and Jesus was born
3. The three magi, Caspar, Melchior and Balthasar, presented their gifts of gold, frankincense and myrrh
4. John the Baptist was a child of the desert
5. Jesus went to hear John preach and presented himself for baptism
6–7. Simon Peter took Jesus up to his house where a great crowd followed and spilled over into the courtyard
8. 'Daughter,' Jesus said to Mary of Magdala, 'your sins are forgiven you'

Baptist has been more dangerous since his death than he was when he was alive.'

Herod well knew this. 'Then don't just stand there,' he said testily, 'tell me what to do.'

The chief of the guard suggested that Jesus should be driven from Galilee, and all the roads except the road to Judea should be closed. 'Let the Imperial Procurator worry about him,' he suggested. But Herod clutched at another idea.

'If he is a prophet,' he said, 'perhaps I should meet him. I should have him perform a miracle – here – in this very room.'

'It might be dangerous,' the chief of the palace guard answered, 'his miracles have a strange effect on people, sometimes changing their entire outlook on life. Does Your Majesty wish to risk such a change?'

'No,' said Herod, 'I want to be safe. Drive him out. And have no mercy on these Zealots. Dispatch them at once.'

The surviving Zealots were dragged from their cells and with their wrists bound above their heads they were tied to a rough wall of planks. At the word of command a line of soldiers hurled javelins at them, and within a short time they were dead.

Simon and Judas were on their way to meet Jesus and the other disciples. Simon received news of the death of the Zealots. He was deeply moved.

'Were they all killed?' asked Judas. 'All of them?'

'All of them,' said Simon. 'They were my brothers. I lived with them since I was a boy.'

Judas put his hand on Simon's shoulder to comfort him. 'I know they were mad,' said Simon, 'I know, but they meant well, how devoted they were! They thought they could force God's hand.'

'You warned them what would happen,' said Judas. 'Poor Amos. To die like that.'

'How good and strong he really was,' said Simon.

'Don't grieve,' urged Judas. 'Jesus will go to Jerusalem

and meet with the Sanhedrin and arrange for action on the plane that his mission demands – with no bloodbath. Come on,' said Judas. 'Let's find the Master.'

The apostles were gathered with Jesus after a frugal meal. Jesus by this time knew that the culmination of his mission was drawing near, and he knew what that culmination would be. So he said to the disciples, 'And who do the people in Galilee say that I am?'

Bartholomew answered, 'Some say, John the Baptist. They won't believe that he is dead.'

'Some know that he is dead, but they think that you are John the Baptist come back to life,' said Andrew. 'Others say you are Elijah back from the grave.' (It was believed that Elijah would return as the forerunner of the Messiah, when the Messiah was about to appear.)

'Others say Jeremiah or Ezekiel,' added Philip. It was the belief that Jeremiah, before Jerusalem was devastated, took the Ark of the Covenant and the Altar of Incense and hid them in a secret cleft in Mount Nebo, and that he would return to bring them out before the Messiah was due.

Then Jesus said, 'And who do you say that I am?'

Judas was ready to give the right answer at once but he left it to Peter to speak, and while the rest hesitated Peter came in strongly, 'I say you are the Christ, the Son of the Living God.'

Jesus answered, 'You are indeed blessed, Simon Barjona, for it was no human being who revealed this to you; it was my Father who is in heaven. I tell you, you are Peter – the man whose name means a rock – and on this rock I will erect my Church, and the powers of death will be helpless to harm it. I will give you the keys of the Kingdom of Heaven, and whatever you forbid on earth will be forbidden in heaven, and whatever you allow on earth will be allowed in heaven. To you all I say this: that Peter has spoken the truth, and now you know what it is. But you must not reveal it to any man. The time is not yet come for that. It will come, for the time is here for me to go to Jerusalem.'

Simon the Zealot looked doubtfully at Jesus, but Judas was cheerful at the prospect of going to Jerusalem.

'Yes, Master,' he said, 'you must go to Jerusalem. The whole city awaits you. The Elders of Israel must know and recognize you.'

Jesus looked very keenly into Judas's eyes. 'No, Judas,' he said, 'in Jerusalem the Son of Man will be rejected by the Elders and the Chief Priests of the Temple, and unbelievers will scourge him, mock him, murder him. Then after three days he will rise again.' The disciples looked at him in horror.

There came a day when Jesus delivered his most famous sermon to the disciples and others who had gathered around him. We call it the Sermon on the Mount. Jesus said:

'O the bliss of those who realize
    the destitution of their own lives,
for the blessings of the Kingdom of Heaven
    are theirs here and now.
O the bliss of those whose sorrow is sore,
    for they shall find courage and comfort.
O the bliss of those whose strength is in their gentleness,
    for they shall enter into possession of the earth.

O the bliss of those who hunger and thirst
    for all that sets them right with God,
    for they shall be satisfied to the full.
O the bliss of those who treat others with mercy,
    for they shall be treated with mercy.

O the bliss of those who are pure in heart,
    for they shall see God.
O the bliss of those who make men friends with each other,
    for they shall be ranked as the sons of God.
O the bliss of those who are persecuted
    for their loyalty to God's way of life,
for the blessings of the Kingdom of Heaven
    are theirs here and now.

Yours is this bliss,
when men shall heap their insults on you,
   and persecute you,
      and tell every wicked kind of lie about you
      for my sake.
When that happens,
rejoice and exult in it,
for you will receive a rich reward in heaven,
   for it was thus that they persecuted
   the prophets who lived before you.

Just so, your light must shine
   for everyone to see, so that,
when they see the lovely things you do,
   it may make them want to praise
   your Father who is in heaven.

But I tell you
   not to resist evil, but,
      if anyone slaps you on the right cheek,
      let him slap you on the other as well;
if anyone asks you for anything,
   give it to him,
and do not refuse anyone
   who wishes to borrow from you.

You must be perfect as
   your heavenly Father is perfect.

Don't make a habit of judging others,
   if you do not want to be judged yourselves.
For the verdict which you pass on others
   will be the verdict that is passed on you.
You will get in exactly the same proportion
   as you give.'

John said: 'How can we, imperfect as we are . . . ?' Jesus
said:

68

'Keep on asking,
   and you will get;
keep on seeking,
   and you will find;
keep on knocking,
   and the door will be opened for you.
For everyone who keeps on asking
   gets what he asks for;
he who keeps on seeking,
   finds;
if a man keeps on knocking,
   the door will be opened.
Is any of you likely to give his son a stone,
   if he asks for a loaf?

Is he likely to give him a snake,
   if he asks for a fish?
If then, evil and ungenerous as you are,
   you know how to give your children good gifts,
how much more can you depend on your Father in heaven,
   to give good things to those who ask him for them?'

At the same time Jesus taught his disciples a prayer,
which we still call the Lord's Prayer.
   'So, when you pray, pray like this:

Our Father in heaven,
May your name be held in reverence,
   May your Kingdom come,
May your will be done,
   as in heaven, so on earth.
Give us today our bread for the coming day.
Forgive us for our failures in our duty to you,
   as we have forgiven those who have failed
   in their duty to us.
Do not submit us to any time of testing,
   but rescue us from the Evil One.'

Into the Sermon on the Mount Jesus put the very essence of his teaching.

That very night Jesus was sitting quietly looking into a small fire, still awake. All the rest of the disciples were asleep, except Peter. Peter approached Jesus. 'Master,' he said.

'Yes?' said Jesus.

'You said,' Peter reminded him, 'that you are going to Jerusalem and that in Jerusalem they will kill you.'

'Yes,' said Jesus.

'If that is true,' Peter said, 'it is our duty to keep you from going. We must not allow it to happen.'

Jesus rebuked him. 'Peter,' he said, 'you are thinking as men think, not as God thinks. The devil is speaking through you.' Then Jesus stood up and said to Peter, 'Get behind me, Satan.'

Shortly afterwards Jesus and his men set out on the fateful last journey to Jerusalem. Jesus's face was set and determined as he moved at the head of his little band along the road, but his followers, remembering his warning of what awaited him there, were apprehensive and downcast. James and John were at the rear of the party.

'One more halt,' James said, 'and we shall be nearly there.'

'And Jerusalem will be swarming with pilgrims up for the Passover,' John answered. 'What will he say to them now, I wonder? And will he go straight into the city and start preaching?'

James shook his head. He had no idea what was going to happen. 'He prophesied that he will suffer death there,' he said.

And Peter, who overheard him, interjected, 'Then let us go, that we may die with him.'

As the group moved on, Jesus striding purposefully in front, the others lagging a little way behind, a man on horseback came riding swiftly toward them from the direction of Jerusalem. Reaching the travellers he dismounted, and having made eager inquiry of the disciples, hurried up to Jesus.

'Master,' he said, 'Martha and Mary, the sisters of your friend Lazarus in Bethany, have sent me to find you. Lazarus is dying.'

'My poor friends!' said Jesus, 'I will go to them. Return and tell them I shall be coming.'

'We must mend our pace if we are to be there in time,' said Peter, who with the other disciples had gathered round during the conversation.

'No, Peter,' said Jesus. 'There is no pressing hurry. We shall arrive in three days' time. This illness will not end in death, but will reveal the glory of God; and through it the Son of Man will be glorified.'

In due time Jesus and his men reached the street in Bethany where Lazarus lived. Martha, who must have been on the watch, ran out to meet them. She was clearly deeply distressed. When she reached him, Jesus took her by the hand. 'It is too late, Lord,' she said. 'If only you had been here my brother would not have died.'

'Your brother,' said Jesus, 'will rise again.'

'I know that he will rise at the last day,' said Martha.

Then Jesus said, 'I am the resurrection and the life. In death to believe in me is to live again. In life, for any man, to believe in me is never to die. Do you believe this?'

Martha answered, 'Yes. I believe that you are the Christ, the Son of God, he who was to come into the world'.

'Where have you laid him?' Jesus asked.

'Come and see,' said Martha.

So they came to the village burial place. The tomb of Lazarus was in a cave, with a stone placed across the opening. Jesus, with Martha and the disciples, stood before the tomb. Mary was there with some other mourners, and Mary was weeping. When she saw Jesus, she knelt at his feet. 'Lord,' she said, 'I prayed and prayed for you to arrive. You would have kept Lazarus from dying.'

Jesus raised Mary to her feet and put his arm around her. He came near to the tomb. He was deeply moved. Jesus wept.

'See how he loved him,' said one of the bystanders.

'He opened the eyes of a blind man,' said a second. 'Could he not have prevented this man's death?'

'Take away the stone,' Jesus said. Some men started to obey when Mary broke in, 'He has been dead for four days. His body must already be decaying.'

'Did I not tell you,' said Jesus, 'that if you believed you would see the glory of God?'

The stone was now removed. People were expecting the stench of decay. It did not come. Jesus fell into deep prayer. Then he lifted up his eyes to heaven. 'Father,' he said, 'I thank you for hearing my prayer. I knew indeed that you always hear me, but I speak for the sake of all those who stand round me, so that they may believe that it was you who sent me.' The entrance to the tomb was dark. There was a long pause and all eyes were fixed on the opening in the rock.

Jesus stood up and called in a loud voice, 'Lazarus, come out!' There was a deep silence. Suddenly there was a glimpse of something white stirring in the gloom of the cave. The patch of white grew gradually larger. Lazarus, his body and limbs swathed in grave clothes and his head bandaged, appeared in the entrance to the tomb. He moved slowly out of the darkness into the light. 'Loose him,' said Jesus, 'and let him go.'

Martha and Mary, trembling, went to their brother and began by uncovering his face. Lazarus opened his eyes. His face was that of one who has been beyond death and is then summoned back to life, and after a moment his eyes came to rest on Jesus.

Jesus said, 'I am the resurrection and the life. In death to believe in me is to live again. In life, for any man, to believe in me is never to die'.

The incident was awesome to those who witnessed it. Everyone was overwhelmed. And it was to have a marked effect on the reception Jesus was to receive in Jerusalem.

The Road to Calvary

Zerah was young, a much respected intellectual, and very ambitious. A member of the Sadducees, he was also a priest of the Temple, and it was through him that Judas made contact with the Establishment. He and Zerah met first in one of the Temple rooms.

'I am extremely flattered,' said Zerah, 'that you have asked to see me. Why did you pick me out, by the way?'

'There are many in Israel who think your influence in the Sanhedrin affords great hope for the future,' replied Judas. 'Since the matter I wish to lay before the High Priest is of the utmost importance for the future of Israel, as well as of immediate urgency, I could think of no better approach to His Highness than through you. You have a reputation for adroitness in practical affairs in addition to your great reputation as a scholar. With respect, you get things done.'

'Since you know so much about me,' said Zerah smoothly, 'you won't be surprised to learn that I know a good deal about you. And of course we all know a great deal about your Rabbi from Nazareth – miracles of healing – production of vast quantities of food out of thin air – raising the dead – extraordinary! – to put it mildly. But is there not just a chance that his astonishing powers come not from the highest but the lowest possible source: in short, from Satan? How can we be sure? I wish my duties had left me time to see your Jesus for myself.'

'I wish they had,' said Judas. 'You would then need no persuading that he is the one man who can bring peace to Israel.'

'Oh?' said Zerah sharply.

'The Zealots started to realize it,' said Judas, 'and so, you might be surprised to learn, did your own Temple Guards. As for the Romans – they are eminently practical. They would welcome anyone who could pacify the country. And if it were to cost them nothing, so much the better. The Sanhedrin should recognize Jesus as the true Messiah and say to the Romans . . .'

'What', Zerah broke in, 'should we say: "Look, Caesar, we have a new ruler – one from the Royal House of David. One in whom we have every confidence, who preaches peace, tolerance and love, even to you Romans. Therefore you may calmly withdraw your troops. We no longer need them . . ."' Judas chose to ignore the irony in Zerah's words.

Zerah looked at him thoughtfully. 'Let us be serious,' he said. 'Judas – is that your name? – you can be a very worthy friend to the Elders of Israel. And they will, I am sure, show their gratitude when the time comes. You said something about the Temple Guards. What did you mean?'

'Like you,' said Judas, 'I have my sources of information. I am not exactly eager to reveal them.'

'All right,' said Zerah, 'you and I should not quarrel. What do you want me to do?'

There was silence for a moment. Then Judas spoke very deliberately. 'Let Jesus of Nazareth prove himself before the Elders of Israel,' he said.

'I think,' said Zerah, 'I can promise you that he will have that opportunity. Meanwhile I shall learn more about him.'

Jesus was about to enter Jerusalem through the Damascus Gate. A vast and highly excited crowd swarmed about the roadway. Judas pushed his way through the jabbering, gesticulating throng, and as he did so he overheard snatches of conversation.

'A great prophet.'

'Greater even than John the Baptist, some say.'

'They say he can raise the dead.'

'They say nonsense then. Nobody can raise the dead.'

'Except God. He can do all things.'

'And didn't he empower Elisha to raise the son of the Shunamite woman from the dead?'

'Glory in the highest! Nothing can resist the power of God's anointed.'

'A new King of the Jews. One who will overthrow our oppressors and rule in equity.'

In their joyful excitement they strewed the roadway with palm leaves and flowers. As he at last came into view a roar of welcome went up, exciting them to still wilder frenzies of enthusiasm.

'Hosanna! Blessed is he that comes in the name of the Lord!'

But there were some to whom his appearance, instead of being a stimulus, acted as a check to enthusiasm. A strange entry this for the rumoured leader who was to overthrow Rome! An emaciated man, riding an ass, preceded by eleven rather ragged supporters.

'Is *this* the new king?' one asked.

'Riding on a donkey!' said another derisively.

But a loud confident voice answered the sneer, 'Zechariah foretold it, "Jerusalem, daughter of Zion, behold thy King cometh unto thee, humble and meek, riding on an ass".'

The acclamations became louder, more joyful than ever as the crowd moved slowly beside and before Jesus, waving their palm leaves, even casting their garments on the roadway for the new king to ride over.

'Hosanna! Blessed is he that comes in the name of the Lord!'

The uproar startled a small group of Sadducees proceeding along a nearby street. They stopped a man who was hurrying past and asked what it meant. 'The prophet, Jesus of Nazareth,' the man said excitedly. 'He is here!'

They let the man go. One of them said, 'There is no great cause for concern,' but they turned and walked after the man toward the source of the disturbance, all the same.

Conveniently stationed at a high window Zerah looked down on the slow-moving procession. He was surprised by the appearance of Jesus, but was more interested in the appearance of Judas, whom he could see, curiously foreshortened, smiling with satisfaction at the way things were going.

When the group of Sadducees arrived on the scene they could not help but be impressed by the enthusiasm of the crowd. Pushing their way to the front they emerged close to Judas. On every side the people were waving, laughing, shouting, 'Blessed be the king that comes in the name of the Lord! Glory in the highest.' One of the Pharisees tried to address the crowd, but realizing the futility of public protest turned angrily to his companions. He had to shout to make himself heard above the acclamations. 'This is sheer fanaticism. Such cries are dangerous. They must be stopped.'

Jesus, as the ass moved slowly forward, overheard the protest. 'If *they* held their peace the very stones would cry out,' he said.

White with anger the Sadducee again turned to his companions. 'Did you ever hear such arrogance?' he cried. 'How dare an upstart Galilean speak thus to a member of the Sanhedrin?'

Progress through the thronging crowd became a snail's crawl, but at length Jesus and the disciples reached the entrance to the Temple, when Jesus dismounted and two of the disciples led away the patient ass. Jesus mounted a few of the Temple steps, and signalled that he wished to speak. His voice rang out.

'The time has come for the Son of Man to be glorified. I tell you, and it is true, if a grain of corn does not fall into the ground and die, it remains alone. But if it dies, it produces a large crop.' The silence of the crowd deepened. Jesus went on, 'It is only for a little while longer that the light is to be with you. Get on your way while you have the light so that darkness may not come down upon you. When a man walks in the dark, he cannot see where he is going. While you have the light, believe in the light, that you may become sons of light.' Then, as if communing with himself, he added, 'I am in distress of soul just now. What am

I to say? Am I to say: "Father save me from this hour?" But no! It is for this purpose that I have come to this hour. Father, glorify your name.' A voice came from heaven, 'I have glorified it already, and I will glorify it again'.

The crowd began shouting again, 'God bless the Son of David. Praise God in the highest heaven. God bless the King of Israel!'

Zerah, who had descended from his observation post as the procession moved on, had made his way to the Court of the Priests by the time it reached the Temple steps. He was discussing the uproar with a small group of priests from among those appointed for the day, who looked to him for a lead. Some of them urged him to intervene at once.

'Intervene?' said Zerah. 'No. At least, not yet. I must confess that I am fascinated by the power of this man over the people. We must try to find out where his power comes from.'

'He is certainly capable of the most astonishing manifestations of power,' said Eliphaz.

'He raised one of his friends from the tomb.'

'A clever trick before coming to Jerusalem', said Jonah.

'You still can't deny that . . .' began Eliphaz, but Zerah broke in, stopping the argument before it developed. 'Please, be advised. Don't act impetuously.' Then he called Eliphaz aside for a private word. 'Eliphaz,' he said, 'would you ask the Captain of the Temple Guard to report to my Lord Caiaphas – immediately.'

Just then, there came a loud outburst from somewhere within the Temple, and the priests hurried out to see what was happening. In the Court of the Gentiles they saw Jesus overturning the tables of the money-changers and driving their owners away. 'It is written,' he said, 'my house is a house of prayer. But you have turned it into a den of thieves.' And after he had finished with the money-changers, he began to drive out the sellers of oxen, sheep and doves for the sacrifices.

To understand his violent reaction to the money-changers

we must remember that Gentiles were not allowed to proceed beyond the first Court, which had become something like an eastern market place. The Temple tax, to which everyone was liable, had to be paid either in Galilean shekels or in shekels of the treasury, since, unlike other coins, these shekels bore no portrait of a ruler. Such portraits were reckoned among the graven images explicitly forbidden by the law of Moses. Hence while Tyrian, Phoenician, Egyptian, Greek and Roman coins would serve for ordinary transactions, they had to be changed into the acceptable shekels to pay the Temple tax. It cost the pilgrim a coin called a *ma'ah* to get his money changed, a *ma'ah* being the equivalent of a new penny. If changing the money involved getting change, the pilgrim had to pay the money-changers another penny for the service. That is to say, he had to pay two new pence (or cents), one to change the money and one to get his change.

As for the sellers of livestock for the sacrifices, what happened was this. You could buy your doves outside the Temple, but they had to pass the scrutiny of inspectors appointed by the Temple authorities. Any animal offered for sacrifice had to be without spot or blemish, and the Temple inspectors were quite certain to find some blemish or some flaw in victims purchased outside. They would thus say to the person seeking an animal to sacrifice, 'You would do best to buy your animal from our stalls, for there they have already been inspected.' This seems harmless enough until it is realized that there were times when a pair of doves cost as little as 5 new pence outside the Temple and as much as 75 new pence inside it. Jesus's wrath was therefore aroused for two reasons. The stalls where the sacrificial victims were sold turned the Temple Court into a market place. What should have been a place of prayer had become a place of noisy bargaining. Secondly, as we have seen, the poor pilgrims were the victims of a swindling racket, and Jesus was unwilling to see any man exploited.

Inevitably, the sensational and spectacular action of Jesus created trouble. The merchants were astonished, afraid and resentful. The priests were shocked. Zerah made an attempt to be conciliatory. He went up to Jesus. 'Rabbi,' he said, 'I am Zerah, a priest of this holy place, and like my brethren, I have followed your mission with interest. We heard good things about you and we were glad. But what you have done here now shocks and surprises us. Do you want to destroy the sacred Temple?'

'The Temple is not mere stone', answered Jesus. 'It is the house of God. It cannot be destroyed so long as God lives there', and as he said it he placed a hand over his own heart. 'Destroy this temple,' he said, 'and in three days I will make it rise again!'

'It took centuries to build this Temple. Do you think you can rebuild it in three days?' Zerah demanded.

'You have said it,' answered Jesus, 'but you have not understood.'

'Rabbi,' said Zerah threateningly, 'I understand better than you think. The Lord Caiaphas will be profoundly interested in all this.' And he went away.

Judas came up to Jesus. 'Master,' he said, 'that Sadducee is one of the most open-minded members of the Sanhedrin. He had every intention of approaching you in a friendly way. He wanted to understand your mission. Was it wise to discourage him?'

Jesus looked at him for a moment in silence, and then in a voice that held both sorrow and pleading said, 'Judas, open your heart, not your mind. Open your heart.'

Jesus was later to preach in the Temple portico, when his hearers included a sprinkling of Sadducees, Pharisees and Zealots, including Barabbas. Despite the opposition of the disciples, some enthusiastic admirers of Jesus brought forward a group of young children, who sang in a far from perfect chorus 'Hosanna to the Son of David'. The Sadducees and Pharisees were incensed by the use of the title.

'You deceive the very children,' Samuel the Sadducee said contemptuously. 'Have you no shame?'

'Have you never read in the psalms,' said Jesus, ' "Out

of the mouths of babes and sucklings thou hast perfected praise"?'

Eliphaz, unable to stand any more, confronted Jesus truculently. 'By what authority do you do these things?' he demanded.

'Before I answer,' Jesus said, 'I will ask *you* a question. From where did John the Baptist receive the authority to baptize, from heaven or from men?'

Samuel the Sadducee began to say, 'From men', but Eliphaz stopped him before he could get the words out. 'You fool!' he whispered. 'Do you want the people to tear you to pieces?'

'So,' said Jesus, 'John's authority was not from men. Then if it was from heaven, why did you not believe him? Answer me.'

There was a silence and then Eliphaz shouted furiously, 'We don't know. We can't tell.'

'John the Baptist,' said Jesus, 'came to you in the way of righteousness, and you did not believe him. Yet there were many sinners who believed. But you, even when you saw that they believed, you did not repent!

'He who believes in me,' said Jesus, 'believes in him who sent me.' The priests and the Pharisees, scowling with anger, went away. Meanwhile Jesus, surrounded by some of his disciples and some of the people who had been listening to him, went towards the Portico of the Ablutions. Barabbas followed with some of his fellow conspirators. They passed two Temple Guards, friends of the Zealots, who kept watch, making sure they were not interrupted. Other people slipped away at the sight of Barabbas who, with only two of his followers, came up to Jesus.

'Master,' he said in low tones, 'I am Barabbas the Zealot. Amos sent us word about you before his murder. The Temple Guards are ready and so are my brothers. We will follow your orders to the end.'

Jesus raised his eyes to Barabbas; 'You have heard that it was said "You shall love your neighbour and hate your enemy". But I say to you, Barabbas, love your enemies and pray for those who misuse and persecute you. The day of forgiveness is upon us.'

'Forgive Herod?' demanded Barabbas incredulously. 'Forgive the Romans?'

Jesus answered simply, 'You must change your hearts'.

Barabbas could not believe his ears. 'The Romans', he said, 'have killed dozens who were not even involved in politics. You can't mean to forgive that, Master. We must meet the sword with the sword.'

'All that take to the sword', said Jesus, 'shall perish by the sword. The new Jerusalem will not be created by armed might, uprisings and murder. The wisdom of God will fill the land as water fills the sea. Barabbas, don't lose your confidence in God. His justice will come down among men, and the lion will lie down with the lamb. There will be no more hurting or destroying, and the voice of weeping shall be heard no more.'

Barabbas and the Zealots were plainly shocked and obviously bitterly disappointed. Jesus stood very close to Barabbas. He addressed him now with a more affectionate voice. He deeply wanted Barabbas to understand. 'I must', said Jesus, 'take on my shoulders the sins of the world. He who would follow me must do the same. The scriptures say, thou shalt not kill. But I say to you, anyone who is angry with his brother without a cause is guilty, and anyone who calls his brother a fool shall be in danger of hell fire.'

Barabbas and his Zealots stared at Jesus as if he was mad. They were incapable of understanding him. Judas's face was troubled. Jesus seemed to have rejected him as well as the Zealots.

The disciples came up to Jesus to tell him that a man was waiting in the hope of seeing him in the Court of the Gentiles, beyond which a Gentile could not come. Jesus went to meet him and found a Roman centurion waiting. The encounter caught the interest of the Roman guards in the Antonia Fortress, who were intrigued to see a centurion respectfully greeting Jesus.

'Lord,' said the centurion, 'I would like to ask you a great favour. I have a servant in my house who is very dear to me, more like a son than a servant. He is very sick, dying I fear. Lord, in all humility I ask . . .'

Jesus broke in, '. . . that I should come to your house? Very well, I will come.' 'No, Lord,' he said, 'I am unworthy that you should enter under my roof. I know that if you say the word my servant will be healed. I am a man who knows all about discipline and authority. I myself have authority over one hundred soldiers, and if I say to one "Do this", I know that he will do it. If I say to another "Go there", I know that he will go. I need not see, I know. So it is enough that you give the word, and it will be done.'

Jesus was deeply moved. He turned to those present and pointed at the centurion. 'Did you hear this man?' he said. 'I say to you all, I have not found faith like this among many in Israel.' Then his gaze, moving over the crowd, fell on the faces of the Pharisees and the Zealots, and they were grim. He laid a friendly hand on the centurion's shoulder. 'Go home,' he said, 'your faith has cured your servant.' The centurion was astonished, not only at the promised miracle, but also that a Jew should voluntarily have touched a Gentile. Barabbas and his Zealots were standing a short way off. For them, that Jesus should have reached out in friendship to touch a Roman soldier was the last straw.

At that moment a very excited crowd entered the courtyard. The Sadducees Ezra, Jonah and Samuel held a terrified young woman in custody. 'No, no,' shouted the young woman, 'let me go!' and on all hands voices were raised. 'Adulteress.' 'Sinner.' 'Kill her!'

Jesus, who had seated himself in a circle of his followers, turned to look at the newcomers. Ezra spoke to him with assumed respect. 'Master,' he said, 'what should we do? This woman has been caught in the act of adultery. She should be punished according to the Law. What do you say?'

Legally, Ezra was right. According to the Law*, the

*Deuteronomy 22:13–24.

penalty for adultery in the case of a betrothed girl was death. She and the guilty partner must be taken outside the city gates and stoned. So, legally speaking, there was only one answer to Ezra's question. 'Answer, Master,' said Eliphaz eagerly, 'we want to know your opinion.' Other voices joined in.

Jesus took his time. He bent down and seemed to be writing with his finger in the dust on the earth. At length he looked up and spoke. 'If anyone among you is without sin, let him throw the first stone.' There was a silence. The woman looked at Jesus with hope. Slowly, the people dropped the stones that they had taken up. Jesus resumed his writing in the dust. The adulteress, freed from the grip of her tormentors, remained motionless, her head bowed down. Jesus looked at her. 'Where are your accusers?' he said. 'Is there anyone who has condemned you?' 'No, Lord,' she answered, 'no one.' Jesus spoke gravely but gently. 'Then neither do I condemn you. Go and sin no more.'

Outside the city gates the Nazareth caravan had just arrived. Among its members were Rabbi Yehuda, now a very old man, and Mary, the mother of Jesus. 'Our feet shall stand within thy gates, O Jerusalem,' Yehuda said. Then to Mary, in a low voice, 'Your son will be teaching in the Temple. Shall I take you to him?' But Mary said, 'No, I will wait. I will see him when it is time.'

The next day a crowd again gathered in the Temple colonnade around Jesus. They were watching him as he anointed the eyes of a blind man with a paste made of dust mixed with spittle.

Unable to see Jesus the blind man called out again. 'Leave my eyes alone! I don't want them touched I tell you.'

Some of the crowd joined in his protest.

'Yes, leave him alone.'

'Why are they smearing that stuff on his eyes? He doesn't want them touched.'

Jesus refrained from answering. He finished anointing

the man's eyes and then, speaking as one with authority, instructed him, 'Go and wash your eyes'.

Surrounded by a number of curious onlookers, the blind man was led off, although most of the people remained behind with Jesus.

Peter asked him, 'Master, the man was born blind, and what I should like to know is this. Who sinned? Did he sin, or was it his father, or his mother?' For it was the Jewish belief that there could be no suffering without sin.

'No one sinned,' said Jesus. 'He was born blind so that the will of God might be made manifest in him. I must perform the work of him who sent me, so long as daylight lasts. Then the night will fall, in which no man may work. But as long as I am in the world, I am the light of the world.'

The blind man went to the pool and washed, and his sight returned. He looked round at the visible world with fear, but with a kind of timid joy also. The crowd began shouting, 'He sees – he's been given his sight! Blind from birth, and now he can see!'

A group of Pharisees tried to check this new wave of popularity for Jesus. When a man shouted, 'How did this happen? How was it done?' a Pharisee turned to the blind man himself and asked, 'And what do *you* say? What do you have to say about the man who healed you?'

'He is a prophet', said the blind man. 'There is no doubt.'

'What are you saying?' said the Pharisee. 'You got your sight back from God, not from that man. He is a sinner.'

The blind man was frightened by the outstretched fists of the Pharisees and shrank back, thus coming close to Jesus, who stood in the midst of his followers. 'Do you believe in the Son of Man?' Jesus asked him quietly.

'Who is he, Master,' said the blind man, 'that I may believe in him?'

'You are seeing him,' said Jesus. 'It is he who is speaking to you.'

'I believe, Lord,' said the blind man.

Whereupon a Pharisee said to Jesus, 'And what is your story – that you can give sight to blind people?'

Jesus addressed the crowd. 'I came into this world to give sight to those who cannot see, and to take away sight from those who can.'

'What do you mean by this?' demanded another Pharisee. 'Do you mean that we who are righteous are blind?'

'If you were blind,' said Jesus, 'you would be without sin, but since you claim to see your sin remains.' 'This man works through the devil!' a Pharisee shouted. 'Why do you listen to him?'

The crowd rapidly increased at the prospect of a row, and began to take sides in the controversy.

'What do you mean – mad?'

'Can the mad restore sight?'

'Can devils make men who are blind see God's daylight?'

'No, it's true – if his power is not from God, it must be from the other one.'

'Shut your ears, don't listen to him!' The Pharisees were succeeding in rousing the crowd against Jesus. The tumult was growing worse. Jesus therefore climbed on to a rock and attacked the group of Pharisees. 'Alas for you, scribes and Pharisees,' said Jesus. 'You hypocrites! You who shut up the Kingdom of Heaven in men's faces, neither going in yourselves nor allowing others to go in. Alas for you, blind guides who strain out gnats and swallow camels. You who bow before the letter of the Law and violate the heart of the Law – justice, mercy, good faith! Alas for you, scribes and Pharisees, you who are like whited sepulchres, fair without, but inside full of dead men's bones and every kind of corruption. Serpents, brood of vipers, how can you escape damnation?'

For some moments Zerah had been an unobtrusive observer of the scene, and at that moment he decided in his heart that Jesus must die. But Jesus had not yet finished. 'Yours is a house of desolation,' he said, 'the home of the lizard and the spider. And this I say to you – you will not see me here again until you have learned to cry with a loud voice "Blessed is he who comes in the name of the Lord!"'

Because I and my father are one and the same.' Zerah was furious.

At these words, there were angry cries.

'Blasphemer!'

'He blasphemed!'

'Stone him!'

'He is a false prophet!'

Other voices were shouting, 'No, he speaks truly!' 'Leave him!' 'Let him go!'

The disciples surrounded Jesus, offering him protection, while the Pharisees incited the crowd against him. 'Seize him!' they shouted. 'Why hesitate? He blasphemes against law and religion. He is a friend of sinners and thieves and whores! From his own mouth he condemns himself. Stone him! Throw him out of the holy city!'

A man in the crowd shouted, 'Throw yourselves out! You whited sepulchres!'

Barabbas emerged from the excited crowd. He shouted, 'Yes, yes, stone the traitor, Caesar's friend, licker of Caesar's feet!' He and his Zealots started throwing stones, and a scrimmage began. A party of Roman guards arrived to restore order, and in the struggle Barabbas seized one of the guards. Some of the Zealots, including Barabbas, were roughly arrested. The Temple party, who had been looking on, hurried away.

Barabbas was marched into the Antonia Fortress and thrown into a cell already occupied by two other Jewish criminals, Joah and Aram. Beyond the fortress Zealots were shouting for his release. Their cries could be faintly heard in the cell and Barabbas, knowing such demonstrations to be useless, listened in stony silence. After a short interval the warden admitted an attendant named Quintus, who was bringing a dish of food and was accompanied by a guard named Quartus.

'Your friends outside want you freed. So that you can carry on with your murdering, I suppose,' Quintus said banteringly.

'I'm not a murderer,' Barabbas protested. 'I'm a patriot,

and shouldn't be in the same cell as that lot,' and he gestured scornfully toward Joah and Aram.

'You're all criminals,' Quintus observed cheerfully, 'and are likely to share the same fate. So don't think you're any different, my fine patriot.'

Towards sunset that evening Jesus and his disciples were in the Garden of Gethsemane on the Mount of Olives. They had withdrawn there because after the riot in which the Zealots had been arrested the city had become dangerous. They were grouped round Jesus, talking quietly, when an elderly Pharisee came up the hill into the garden, plainly seeking for someone. He paused for a moment to regain his breath after the long hill climb. Then he recognized Peter and came over to him.

'You will remember me, Nicodemus. And you know you can trust me. I've come to warn you, and to offer my help. You're in danger, very real danger. Tell your Master to keep out of public places – to keep right out of sight.' Then he picked out Jesus and turned to him.

'Rabbi,' he said, 'there is to be a meeting of the Sanhedrin. You have many enemies there, but friends also who know that you are a teacher come from God, for no man can work your miracles unless God is with him. Yet, my heart is still troubled and my mind confused. You must help me to see the truth.'

'Except a man be born again from above,' Jesus said to Nicodemus, 'he cannot see the Kingdom of God.' 'How can a man be born again?' said Nicodemus, puzzled. 'Can he enter his mother's womb a second time?' Jesus answered. 'I tell you, and it is true, unless a man is born of water and the Spirit, he cannot become a member of the Kingdom of God. Physical birth can only beget a physical creature; but spiritual birth begets a spiritual creature. You must not be surprised that I said to you that you must all be born again from above. The wind blows where it wills, and you hear the sound of it but do not know where it comes from nor where it is going. And there is the same invisible and

87

unpredictable power in everyone who undergoes this spiritual rebirth. The light came into the world but men prefer darkness.'

'How can this be?' asked Nicodemus.

'God so loved the world,' said Jesus, 'that he sent his own son, that whosoever believes in him should not perish but have eternal life. God sent his son into the world not to condemn the world but that it might be saved through him.'

Nicodemus was moved and troubled. 'Master,' he said, 'I beg you, take care. Too many hate you.' In a low voice Jesus quoted, 'He was despised and rejected of men. A man of sorrows and acquainted with grief . . . And we hid as it were our faces from him . . .'

'That's Isaiah, Master,' Nicodemus said.

'Old words,' Jesus said to Nicodemus, 'but not much time will pass before they become new again, and then perhaps you will be reborn.'

The same evening, selected members of the Sanhedrin assembled in a council chamber of the Temple, having been hastily summoned to a very secret meeting. Zerah the Sadducee was present, as were Pharisees Nicodemus and Joseph of Arimathea. The attitude of the members was secretive, almost furtive.

The meeting was presided over by the High Priest, Caiaphas, and he sat leaning forward, his eyes half closed. Although members of the Sanhedrin specifically addressed him, he neither answered nor raised his gaze to attend. He seemed either bored with the business or too absorbed in his own thoughts to take notice. As a consequence everyone redoubled their efforts to attract his attention.

'The city is in uproar,' said Haggai. 'One group of rebels has been arrested already, and more Roman troops are arriving from Caesarea.'

'Our information,' said Samuel, 'is that this Jesus of Nazareth will use the Passover festival to declare himself the Son of David. The mob already calls him a prophet. I appeal to our High Priest Lord Caiaphas . . .'

Joseph of Arimathea broke in, 'I don't believe it. I have seen Jesus. I have heard him preach. He talks of goodness and the virtues of poverty . . .'

'And hence of the vices of the rich and the hypocrisy of the respectable,' Haggai broke in. 'We all know about the virtues of the respectable,' said Joseph of Arimathea. 'We can imagine what a sincere teacher like Jesus must think of them . . .'

'A sincere teacher!' exclaimed Habbakuk, appalled. 'He is a false teacher and is not even original. He says nothing new. We've heard it all before, from John the Baptist, from hundreds of others.'

'Jesus of Nazareth', said Samuel, 'inflames the mob and the Zealots, who regard him as the new King of Israel who can sweep out the Romans.'

'But again and again he says that his kingdom is not of this world,' objected Joseph of Arimathea.

'Indeed he does,' sneered Ezra. 'He merely says *he* is the fulfilment of God's promise. The completion of our entire history. I tell you,' he cried angrily, 'he outrages the law of our Fathers. His guilt is blasphemy.'

The atmosphere was becoming more and more heated, and Nicodemus now spoke. 'I submit with all respect that we must also consider the possibility that Jesus of Nazareth *is* the Messiah awaited by our people.'

The interjection led to a moment of appalled silence.

'A carpenter from Galilee?' shrilled Habbakuk. 'Riding into Jerusalem on a donkey! Just to fulfil the prophecy?'

'Like our brother Joseph,' said Nicodemus, 'I have heard him preach. I was moved and I saw wonders . . . signs that God may be with him.'

'Have a care, Master Nicodemus,' said Habbakuk. 'You have heard only oratory. You have only seen magic that comes from the devil.' 'The coming of the Messiah,' said Nicodemus, 'is the core of our faith. Why should he not come now? Why do we dream that our liberator will be a new Solomon or a new David? Is God not allowed to choose the son of a carpenter from Nazareth? David was a shepherd. Who are we to decide the way in which God should choose to help his people? We are grains of sand. We are chaff blown in the wind. May the Lord God open our eyes to his wisdom.'

Predictably his words produced an angry outcry. 'Who says that Jesus is not dangerous, when people in our very midst defend him?' cried Samuel, and many speakers started shouting in chorus, until they suddenly realized that the High Priest was holding up his hand for silence.

The authority of Caiaphas, like his sincerity, was beyond question. 'Brethren,' he said, 'I am an old man and, like Master Nicodemus, I am deeply troubled. My heart is sore wounded. How can we have reached such divisions and bitterness? This rabbi from Nazareth must be an exceptional man . . .' Habbakuk was about to interrupt but Caiaphas checked him with a gesture. 'Please listen, brethren,' he went on. 'Never before has the Sanhedrin been so divided. Why? How has Jesus of Nazareth managed to do this to us? In what does he differ from other prophets and rabbis of our two thousand years of history? I will tell you, brethren. He differs in that he says that he has the power to forgive sins. We have always believed that only God has the power to do that. What does it then mean if this man Jesus takes to himself the power to forgive sins? I hardly dare utter the thought. It means that a carpenter from Nazareth identifies himself with God. This desperate sin happened only once before. Only one creature dared that, and his name was Lucifer. Brethren! Master Joseph! Master Nicodemus! Can we accept his claim? Can a man be equal to God?' Nicodemus was about to speak, but checked himself and remained silent. 'Our scriptures tell us,' continued Caiaphas, 'that the Messiah will come as a king. Is this man a king? If he is not, is he a blasphemer? What is the truth in him for which we are to reject two thousand years of teaching and endanger the lives of our people? This is the question that devastates my heart. The Romans will not wait long for us to answer. At the first whisper of revolt they will begin slaughtering the people. We cannot allow our people to die for a false Messiah. We must decide, we must act, in haste. If Jesus is a false prophet, should one man die for the good of the people? Should the nation perish for one man?'

'Lord Caiaphas,' Zerah broke in, 'may I remind you with respect that the people of Israel may put a goat to death but not a man.' As an occupied country Israel was not allowed to carry out the death penalty. The Sanhedrin could pronounce a man guilty and condemn him to death but the sentence could be carried out only by the Romans at their own discretion.

'Thank you, Zerah,' said Caiaphas. 'I wondered when I should hear from you. You remind us of the limits to our justice. We may formulate a charge. The Romans must execute it.'

'For us,' said Zerah, 'this Jesus is guilty of blasphemy: for the Romans it would have to be treason.'

'Guilty?' Joseph of Arimathea broke in. 'Do you have proof that he is guilty?'

'Yes,' said Zerah. 'I heard him in the Temple. He claimed to be the Son of God. That merits death.'

'Surely, my Lord,' said Nicodemus, 'the Sanhedrin has always been reluctant to pass death sentences. And does our law condemn a man without first giving him a hearing before the Elders of Israel?'

'No, Master Nicodemus,' answered Caiaphas, 'it does not. We must question the man and give him every opportunity to explain himself.'

The formal part of the meeting was now over, and most of the members left. But at the request of Caiaphas a small group remained to consider how best Jesus could be brought before the Sanhedrin for questioning.

'We must arrest him,' said Zerah.

'No,' said Joseph of Arimathea.

'Let me persuade him,' said Nicodemus.

'We must take him in darkness,' said Zerah, 'to avoid a riot. There are always too many people around him.'

'My Lord?' Nicodemus broke in, but Caiaphas said, 'I would like to follow your advice, Nicodemus, but I believe that Zerah is right.' Zerah was about to leave, but Caiaphas checked him. 'Zerah,' said Caiaphas.

'My Lord?' said Zerah.

'Do not forget that he is one of our brothers.'

It was late when Zerah met Judas, who was standing waiting for him in the Court of Israel. He looked downcast and tired.

'Ah, Judas,' said Zerah. 'I'm glad you came, I've been trying to get in touch with you. You haven't been with the Master for the last day or two. Where have you been?'

'I have been trying to think, Zerah,' said Judas, 'trying to decide what to do.'

'You seemed to me to be a man who was very sure of himself and of what to do,' said Zerah.

'I'm not now,' said Judas. 'I'm confused. I always thought that a sanction from the Sanhedrin could solve everything. I thought that I should think clearly and then act clearly.'

'That's right,' said Zerah, 'a cool head and a strong will.'

'The Master told me,' said Judas, 'that the heart is more important. He doesn't need my ideas. I'm tormented by the fear that he's right. *Have* I hardened my heart? Am I fit to be one of his disciples?' There was a long pause.

'Judas,' said Zerah, 'don't lie to yourself. The truth is that in your heart you no longer believe that Jesus of Nazareth *is* the Messiah. You no longer believe his claim to fulfil the scriptures. You are torn by doubts.' Zerah looked hard at Judas, and Judas's eyes fell before him. 'Judas,' he said, 'there is only one way to know the truth. Hand Jesus over to the Sanhedrin.' Judas looked up. Zerah smiled reassuringly. 'Think, Judas', he said. 'Many influential members of the Council admire Jesus. He will be fairly judged. If he is the Messiah God will not abandon him. If he is not . . . if he is only another false prophet . . . you and I will have saved Israel.' There was a silence while the two men looked at each other. Then Zerah said as he turned away, 'The San-hedrin will be very grateful to you.'

The Passover was the greatest of the annual festivals which every adult male who lived within fifteen miles of Jerusalem had to attend. Its origin went back to the supreme moment in the national history, when a reluctant Pharaoh was compelled by a succession of disastrous plagues to allow the enslaved Israelites to go free. Time and again Pharaoh 'hardened his heart', until a last and most terrible plague broke his resistance. The angel of death passed through the land and slew the firstborn of every Egyptian house-hold.

Warned by God of the visitation in advance, the Israelites were ordered to dip a bunch of hyssop into the blood of a newly slain lamb, and smear the doorposts and lintels of their houses. When the angel of death saw the blood he would 'pass over' the house, leaving its inmates unscathed; hence the name of the feast, which is still celebrated by the Jews on the 14th day of Nisan (approximately 14th April).

Many symbolic ingredients made up the feast, and were consumed in the course of an impressive ritual which included prayer, the singing of psalms, and the recital of the history of Israel up to the great deliverance.

Wine was taken at four stages in the meal, as a reminder of the four promises of God concerning delivery from bondage, and the unique status of the Israelites as the chosen people.

Bread was broken as a reminder that slaves had only broken crusts to eat, never a whole loaf.

Bitter herbs placed between two pieces of unleavened bread recalled the bitterness of slavery and the bread their fathers had eaten when escaping from Egypt. These were dipped into the *charosheth*, a paste made of dates, apples, nuts and pomegranates to symbolize the clay of which their enslaved fathers had been compelled to make bricks. The dipped bread was called the sop.

The chief ingredient of the feast was of course the whole

lamb, a reminder of the slain lamb whose sprinkled blood preserved Jewish households when the angel of death passed through Egypt. A minimum of ten celebrants was required at the festival in any one house, and whatever remained of the lamb had to be destroyed. It must not be kept over and used at an ordinary meal.

This was the Passover Feast which Jesus took and made his own. The two parts which he must have made specially his own were the breaking of bread and the cup of wine. To this part of the ceremony Jesus added his own explanation. He must have said something like this; 'Blessed art thou, O Lord our God, who has blessed us with thy laws and made bread issue from the earth.' Then he must have gone on, 'From this moment this bread will no longer be the bread of the passage of our fathers from bondage to freedom. For this is my body, which enters into death for you. From this moment on, do this in remembrance of me. This Passover, memorial of the bondage in Egypt, is for you today the passage from the bondage of death to the freedom of life. This is the bread of life. Whoever eats of this bread shall have eternal life.'

Clearly, a new revelation was given to the apostles in these words.

Then Peter said, 'Lord, we are happy to eat this Passover with you.'

And Jesus answered gravely, 'Truly, I tell you, one of you is about to betray me.' The disciples were torn between consternation and disbelief. Peter expressed their dismay.

'I speak for us all, Master, when I say that none here could as much as dream of betraying you. Do you mean that evil will take possession of one of us?'

'I know those whom I have chosen,' said Jesus, 'but the scripture must be fulfilled.'

John, who was sitting next to Jesus, whispered to him, 'Lord, tell me who will betray you.' And Jesus whispered back, 'He who dips his bread in the plate when I dip mine.'

Just then, Judas dipped his bread in the *charosheth*. John looked in horror, but he kept silent. And Jesus said quietly,

'Judas, what you are going to do, do it quickly.' Thereupon Judas got up and went out.

An apostle asked his neighbour, 'Where is he going?' And his companion answered, 'The Master told him to do something.'

Then came the last cup of the feast. As Jesus raised it he said, 'Now the son of man is risen and enters into glory. All will be gathered unto him. I shall not be with you much longer. You will look for me . . . but where I am going, you cannot come.'

At this Peter was unable to restrain himself. 'Master,' he said, 'I will follow you wherever you go.'

'No, Peter,' said Jesus, 'now you cannot follow me. You will follow me later. Truly, I tell you, all of you will abandon me.'

'Never, never, I swear,' said Peter, 'never. Why do you say such things? I will never deny you.'

'Peter,' Jesus said, 'before the cock crows tomorrow you will have denied me three times. Remember my words.'

'Never,' Peter cried again, 'never!'

Jesus looked round his disciples. 'If I do not leave,' he said, 'the Holy Spirit cannot descend upon you. Greater love hath no man than this, that a man lay down his life for a friend. By this shall all men know that you are my disciples, if you love one another. I am the way, the truth and the life. From now on the cup will not only be a memorial and sacrament of the covenant that God made with our fathers on Mount Sinai. This cup which is poured out for you is the new covenant in my blood. Do this in memory of me. You will thus share my death and my resurrection. As the branch cannot bear fruit by itself, but only as it abides in the vine, so neither can you unless you abide in me. I am the vine. You are the branches. He who abides in me, and I in him, he it is who bears much fruit, for apart from me you can do nothing.' The emotional atmosphere became more intense as Jesus, looking upward, said, 'Father, the hour has come. Glorify thy son, that the son may glorify thee. Thou hast given him power to give eternal life, which is to know thee, the only true God, and Jesus Christ whom thou hast sent. Father, keep in thy name those whom thou hast given me. Sanctify them in the truth. Thy word is truth. As thou didst send me into the world, so I have sent them into the world that hates them. For their sake, I consecrate myself, that they also may be consecrated in truth. I do not pray for these only, but also for all who believe in me through their word, that they may all be one, even as thou, Father, art in me and I in thee, so also may they be in us, that the world may believe that thou hast sent me.'

The meal was drawn to its close with the quiet singing of the 136th Psalm, and anxiety and sadness were for the moment forgotten in the fervency of prayer.

After the meal Jesus led his disciples to the Garden of Gethsemane. The garden was an orchard enclosed on two sides by a high wall, with the other two sides bounded by a deep ravine. There was almost a full moon, and its brilliancy lit up the scene as though it were daylight. Jesus and the apostles approached the orchard, and a boy named Mark opened a little gate in the wall to admit them and remained on watch by the gate after they had entered.

Jesus spoke to the disciples. 'The hour is near when you

9. Lazarus, his body and limbs swathed in grave clothes and his head bandaged, appeared in the entrance to the tomb

10–11. 'Behold the King cometh unto thee, humble and meek, riding on an ass'

12–13. 'This is the bread of life. Whoever eats of this bread shall have eternal life'

14. Pilate's sign had gone up over the cross, 'Jesus of Nazareth, King of the Jews'

15. His mother looking at his lifeless, rainwashed body gave vent to a terrible flood of grief

16. *above* 'Peter, Matthew, all of you!' cried Mary Magdalene, 'I've seen him. I've seen the Master!'
below The disciples turned to look and Jesus stood there silhouetted in the doorway

shall all be scattered, each on his own, and you will leave me.'

'Lord,' Peter said, 'I am ready to follow you to the death.'

'Three times, Peter,' said Jesus, 'before the first cock crows. Remember. My soul is heavy with sorrow, even unto death. Keep watch while I pray.'

He went forward a little way and dropped on his knees. The apostles were uncertain whether to go with him, but Peter, with a gesture, bade them stop.

Then Jesus prayed, 'My God, my God, why hast thou forsaken me? I call thee by day and thou dost not answer, by night and I have no peace. Do not stay far from me, as my anguish is near and none can help me.' He fell on his face. Andrew, John and Peter were watching. Andrew exclaimed, 'Look at the – sweat?' John said, 'It's not sweat. It's . . .' Peter exclaimed, 'Oh, my dear Lord!'

Jesus continued in anguished prayer, and the disciples, their eyes heavy with watching, fell asleep. At length Jesus stood up. The bright moonlight showed the boy Mark by the gate, also asleep, and a shadow passed over him. Then Jesus went up to Peter and laid his hand on his shoulder to waken him. 'So,' he said, 'you had not the strength to keep awake with me for one hour. The spirit is willing, but the flesh is weak.' Peter, startled, shook the others awake. 'Behold,' said Jesus, 'the hour has come when the Son of Man is to be betrayed into the hands of sinners.'

The wind was rising and clouds appeared in the sky. From beyond the wall there was a sound of voices. 'Wake up, boy,' a guard called roughly. 'Let us through.'

'There's no one here,' said Mark, terrified.

'So much the better,' said the guard's voice, 'but we shall see.'

'Let go! Let me go! Help!' the boy shouted.

The disciples were thrown into disorder. 'What's happening?' they called to one another. 'We've been betrayed.'

'These men are not Romans.'

'Quick, there may be a gate on the other side.'

Some of the apostles ran across the clearing, then they stopped and returned, realizing that Jesus had not moved and that Peter, John and Matthew were retracing their steps and going back to him. A group of men guided by Judas appeared in the garden. Judas went straight up to Jesus and kissed him on the cheek. 'Master,' said Judas.

Jesus stared at him. 'This is your hour, Judas,' he said, 'the hour of shadows. You betray your Master with a kiss.' Judas looked at him, confused and troubled.

Zerah pointed out Jesus to the guards. 'That's the man,' he said. 'Arrest him.'

The guards moved forward to seize Jesus. Andrew and Peter threw themselves on Judas. 'You planned this. You dog. You traitor. You planned it from the start!' Andrew struck Judas on the face.

Judas, with the strength of despair, held Andrew by the wrists. 'You ignorant fisherman! Why can't you use your brains.' He pushed Andrew away and grabbed Peter. 'Peter,' he pleaded, 'listen. Surely you can understand that if he is the Messiah he will triumph. The only way to help him is to force him to speak to the Sanhedrin. He has friends there. Let them escort him to Caiaphas.'

'Never!' cried Peter. 'If they take him, he won't come back.'

'Peter', said Judas. 'Do you really believe in him?' But Peter had turned to attack the guards, who had already bound Jesus's wrists. He gave one guard's ear a glancing wound with his knife. Jesus in a commanding voice stopped him. 'No, Peter,' he ordered, 'put your dagger down.'

Peter was perplexed by the calmness of Jesus. He began to think that just possibly what Judas had said was true. There was a moment of great confusion. Zerah called for the other guards who had remained outside the wall. 'Arrest them all!'

Jesus checked him. 'It was me you sought,' he said. 'Now you have found me, let them go!' In a moment the garden, the scene of so much commotion, was almost deserted. The disciples ran away. Jesus was marched out by the guards,

Zerah leading.

Once they had gone, the disciples, slowly and furtively, began to emerge from their hiding places. They drew together, confused and frightened.

'They were Temple Guards,' Philip whispered.

'They'll have taken him to the High Priest,' Matthew added.

'Judas,' muttered Andrew, 'said it was to save him.'

'*He said!*' John interjected. 'He was the betrayer. The Master knew he was betraying him.'

'Nicodemus warned us,' Peter said bitterly. 'He warned us.'

'We had better separate,' Philip said. 'Some of us should go and find out where he is.'

'We must remember to keep well out of sight,' said Matthew. 'We are all in danger now.'

'No, I am going after the Master,' said Peter. 'What Judas said might be true.'

Very early the next morning, Judas, desperately agitated, entered the courtyard of Caiaphas's house. A guard opened a door and looked out through the crack. Judas shouted to the guard, 'Where have they taken him? Where's Zerah? I must speak with Zerah the priest'. He saw the door closing and rushed over to it. He beat on it with his fists. The guard opened the door slightly and looked out again. 'Is he here?' demanded Judas. 'Did they bring him here? Call the priest for me, Zerah.'

The first man called to a second guard who was in the courtyard, 'Here, throw him out!' He closed the door and the guard in the courtyard approached Judas. 'You hear,' he said. 'Get out.' He tried to get hold of Judas to throw him out and Judas cried out again, 'I must speak to Zerah. Don't you understand? Make him come out to me.'

The main door of the house opened and Zerah stepped out followed by a group of priests and a guard. He walked through the door at which Judas had been knocking minutes before. Judas ran up to him. 'Zerah,' he said, 'at last. Where is the meeting with the Lord Caiaphas? I must be there with Jesus.'

'Meeting?' said Zerah. 'There is no meeting.'

'What?' cried Judas.

'There's an investigation,' said Zerah. 'Your Jesus had to answer many questions.'

Judas stared at him in horror. 'I did wrong,' he said, 'to deliver him to you. His blood is innocent.'

Zerah answered, 'You helped Israel, Judas. You deserve our gratitude.' He started to leave but stopped and turning with an apologetic smile put a bag of money into Judas's hands. 'I hope,' he said, 'you won't be offended by this. This is for your services.' And he walked away quickly, followed by his men.

Judas remained standing motionless, the bag in his hand.

'That's enough now,' said the guard. 'You've got what you wanted, haven't you? So now get out of here,' and he seized Judas by the arm.

There was a frenzied knocking at the door of Joseph of Arimathea's house. The door opened and Joseph looked out anxiously. It was Rabbi Yehuda, the Nazareth rabbi, who was knocking, while Mary stood a little way off. The two men spoke rapidly, in great agitation.

'I am sorry,' said Rabbi Yehuda, 'to waken you at this hour.'

'I was up,' answered Joseph.

'Jesus of Nazareth has been arrested,' Rabbi Yehuda said. 'His mother and I . . .'

Joseph of Arimathea broke in, 'I know! I have been summoned to a meeting. I will do everything I can.'

Men by this time were running through the streets of Jerusalem. Judas ran along frantically. Joseph of Arimathea was also hurrying to the High Priest's house. Peter was slinking furtively along by a wall inside the city.

In the country outside Jerusalem the pale light of the early sun threw long shadows. It cast one shadow which moved rhythmically, forwards then backwards. Some coins glinted on the ground and seemed in their brightness to be greeting the morning light. The returning shadow dimmed their brightness for a moment then let them shine again as the body of Judas, suspended from the tree, swung lazily to and fro.

PART 6

The Prophecy Fulfilled

Daylight would not be long in coming now.

The servants and Temple Guards standing round the fire in the courtyard to Caiaphas's house, watched with idle interest as members of the Sanhedrin hurried up to the great portico, some importantly, others with tense anxious faces.

In the house, in the servants' hall, a detachment of soldiers with time on their hands and Jesus at their mercy had invented a mocking game. Having blindfolded the prisoner they one by one crept up and punched him, now here now there, then to roars of appreciative laughter they called out, 'Prophesy now, who hit you?'

The rough sport was interrupted by the entrance of Zerah. He looked on coldly for a few minutes, then, without a word being spoken, a soldier stepped forward and removed the blindfold. 'You can untie his hands too,' Zerah snapped. When the order had been carried out he indicated with a curt jerk of his head that Jesus was to follow him. With similar terse signalling he told off four of the Temple Guards to accompany them, and led the way out through the servants' entrance across the courtyard to the great portico.

Peter had made his way into the courtyard, and was feeling isolated, lonely, chilly, and decidedly out of his depth in the precincts of the great house and in the company of its knowing retainers. With a clutch of fear he saw Jesus emerge with the soldiers and pass silently across the courtyard, to disappear again into the great house. He started to shiver and began to edge his way toward the fire.

Zerah led his small party until they reached an imposing assembly room. Here Caiaphas was seated, flanked on one side by Sadducees and on the other by Pharisees, among whom were Nicodemus and Joseph of Arimathea. Zerah placed Jesus, standing, before the High Priest, with a Temple Guard on either side. These arrangements completed, he took his place at the table, next to the High Priest.

It was an investigation they were conducting, not a formal trial, and the approach of Caiaphas was at the beginning quite disarming. 'Rabbi,' he said to Jesus, 'we have brought you here so that you can answer for yourself. There have been charges of blasphemy. Remembering that, we want you to think very carefully before answering our questions. And the first question, indeed the key question, is simply this: What is the nature of the doctrine that you and your disciples have been spreading here in Judea?'

'My Lord Caiaphas,' Jesus answered, 'I have spoken openly for all the world to hear. I have taught daily in the Temple where Jews from the whole country meet together. I have said nothing in secret. Those who have heard me are my witnesses.'

At this display of firmness one of the guards, hoping to ingratiate himself with his superiors by a show of righteous indignation, aimed a blow at Jesus. 'Is that the way to answer the High Priest?' he demanded.

Nicodemus at once protested. 'My Lord,' he cried, 'the man exceeds his duty. His conduct is most unseemly. Most unseemly.'

'I agree', said Caiaphas. 'His action was quite unwarranted,' and turning to the guard he said, 'You are dismissed. Leave the council chamber.' Surlily crestfallen the man went out. Another guard stepped into his place and Caiaphas turned again to Jesus. 'Please continue, Rabbi,' he said courteously.

'If I have done anything wrong,' said Jesus, 'make a charge against me. If I have not, then why am I being held?'

His defiant attitude disturbed his friends, and seeing their anxiety his opponents became more assured. They began to press charges.

'My Lord Caiaphas,' Haggai the Sadducee called out in a loud assertive voice. 'There are witnesses who will testify that he said he would destroy the Temple and build it again in three days.'

'I heard him myself,' confirmed Zerah, speaking in low confidential tones to the High Priest.

'But no man could say such a thing and mean it literally,' Nicodemus objected. 'Whatever was said about rebuilding the Temple must have had a symbolic meaning.'

'No, no, and again no!' another Pharisee cried excitedly. 'He said he would destroy the Temple, and those who heard him knew that he meant exactly what he said. He would destroy the Temple. Then after four days he would rebuild it.'

'Three days? Four days?' said Joseph of Arimathea. 'The witnesses disagree.'

'How can we remember every last detail!' said Haggai. 'There was a riot which Jesus himself provoked, but for which the Romans will hold us responsible.'

'The riot,' Nicodemus reminded him, 'was caused by Barabbas.'

'But Barabbas was provoked to violence by the shocking blasphemy of the accused,' said Zerah. 'Who can say how many more devout Jews he will provoke by his preaching? And every disturbance provides the Romans with another excuse to attack our people.'

'Yes, we all know what the Romans have done to our people,' said Joseph of Arimathea. 'Our people have been nailed to the very walls of Jerusalem because there were not scaffolds enough to satisfy the Roman lust for blood. We cannot enter our holy city without the stench of Jewish victims assaulting our nostrils. Let us indeed think carefully about the way the Romans treat our people. Do any of us here wish to give Pontius Pilate another victim if we can prevent it?'

'I must revert to my former question,' said the High Priest. 'What exactly is the nature of our brother's teaching?' They all looked at Jesus. The crucial moment had come.

With great solemnity Caiaphas addressed him. 'In the name of the living God, I adjure you to tell us if you are indeed the Christ, the Son of God.'

Jesus answered, 'I am'.

The reply was so sensational that it stunned the whole assembly into momentary silence. His friends were utterly dismayed. He had himself deliberately closed the door of hope. His enemies, though appalled by his blasphemy, were secretly delighted by his folly. The claim, so openly made, was so unequivocal that there could now be no escape. They could proceed against him with a good conscience and with every prospect of attaining their end.

From every side cries of 'Blasphemy' and 'Away with him' went up. 'We need hear no more,' said Caiaphas, but Jesus had not finished.

'And you shall see the Son of God sitting at the right hand of the Power of God and coming in the clouds of heaven,' he said.

Caiaphas rose and solemnly rent his priestly robe, whether ceremonially at the blasphemy, or in despair at Jesus's obstinacy, those who witnessed the act could not decide. Zerah, anxious to take immediate advantage of the situation, gave them no time to reflect. 'We have all heard him,' he said in rapid, decisive tones. 'He has condemned himself. For such blasphemy there can be but one penalty. Death. We must take him to Pilate to have the death penalty confirmed. But first we must formulate suitable charges against him. Take him away,' he said, turning to the guards, 'and hold him in safe custody.'

Jesus was accordingly taken out and led back, through the courtyard to the soldiers' quarters. Peter, who had edged his way cautiously right up to the fire, and was warming himself with the servants, once more saw Jesus silently pass. Something in his look as his eyes followed Jesus arrested the attention of one of the maidservants. 'You were with him, weren't you?' she asked.

'No,' declared Peter, in a sudden fright, 'I have no idea what you're talking about.' And he heard a cock crow.

'You speak like someone from Galilee,' said another maid, her curiosity aroused. 'Surely you must be one of his disciples.'

Peter's voice grew strident. 'I've already told you I know nothing whatever about the man', and he began calling down curses on himself if he was not telling the truth. And again the cock crew.

The maid stared at him. Tears forced themselves into his eyes. He rushed from the courtyard and his weeping became uncontrollable.

And for the third time the cock crew.

It was always a matter of keen regret for Pilate to have to leave the civilized comforts and amusements of Caesarea, his Roman capital for the administration of Palestine, to take up residence in the dreary Jewish capital. At Passover time especially, Jerusalem was at its fanatical worst, and as he reached the outskirts of the city his gloom and irritability increased.

Once inside the fortress Pilate lost no time in reaching the comfort of his private apartments. He was welcomed by Quintilius, the Deputy Procurator and fortress commander responsible for order in Jerusalem.

'Who is this Barabbas?' Pilate asked, 'the mob yelled his name at me on my way here.'

'He was arrested for public disaffection,' Quintilius answered. 'His death warrant awaits your signature.'

'What was his crime?'

'He is a Zealot. He smashed a Roman standard and killed one of our auxiliaries.'

'Is he popular?' Pilate asked.

'Very, with the Jewish rabble.'

'A friend of the Sanhedrin?' Pilate asked.

'Far from it', said Quintilius.

'Can we use the incident to our advantage?'

'It is customary to release a prisoner in celebration of the Passover.'

'Should Barabbas be the man?' asked Pilate.

'Are you tired of the stench of executions?' asked Quintilius.

'Should Barabbas be the man?' Pilate repeated irritably.

'I am coming to that,' said Quintilius. 'Interestingly enough Barabbas had been roused by the words of a fanatical preacher, Jesus of Nazareth.'

'What makes that interesting?' demanded Pilate.

'Jesus has himself been seized by the Sanhedrin and sent to us for execution on a charge of blasphemy.'

'Blasphemy?' said Pilate. 'I am not interested. The Jewish religion bores me. Their blasphemer can wait.'

'The Jews I have spoken to said our charge would have to be one of treason.'

'Are you saying that it would be more expedient to release the preacher?'

'That will be for Your Excellency to decide. The preacher himself appears to be harmless enough, but his preaching seems to anger violent extremists, like Barabbas. If he was released his preaching might bring more of them into the open, when we could deal with them. On the other hand the release of a blasphemer might dismay the Sanhedrin more than the release of a Zealot.'

Pilate reflected a moment. 'It is a complicated business', he said. 'In your opinion, what is the most important consideration?'

'The goodwill of Rome', answered Quintilius.

'Rome?' queried Pilate. 'What does that mean? Rome?'

'With every respect, Your Excellency, I mean that if disorders continue despite so many executions, Rome might consider Your Excellency responsible.'

Pilate wanted to lose his temper but controlled himself. 'You think Barabbas is a ringleader, and if we could use the preacher to induce a few more of the ringleaders to betray themselves, things would quieten down?'

Quintilius inclined his head.

'I will see these Jews,' Pilate said. 'Send them to the trial room.'

'I regret, Your Excellency,' said Quintilius, 'that we must

go out to them.'

'What?' Pilate exclaimed.

'They refuse to enter,' said Quintilius. 'They are exceedingly firm. It has to do with their religious scruples. They would be defiled by entering the house of a heathen.'

'What a people!' exclaimed Pilate. 'I despise and detest the lot of them.'

He would, he decided, be in no hurry to meet these fanatical representatives of the Sanhedrin. If they wouldn't come in neither would he go out, not until it suited him. At length, however, supported by Quintilius, he made his appearance. He assumed a bored, indifferent air as though their affairs were too trivial to concern him.

'You well know,' he said, 'that I am not concerned with infractions of the law of your religion. My function is political and administrative.'

'We know that, Your Excellency,' said Haggai, who was a chosen speaker for the deputation. 'But this man perverts our religion. If he were not an evil-doer we would not have brought him to you.'

'He says he is the Christ,' enlarged Zerah, 'meaning the anointed one.'

'Thank you,' said Pilate, 'I do know some Greek.'

'The anointed state refers expressly to kingship,' Haggai explained. 'Therefore in claiming to be the anointed one Jesus was claiming to be King in Israel – a claim we utterly deny.'

Pilate ignored their inferences about the anointed one. 'Has he ever incited the people to overthrow Rome?' he asked.

Haggai and Zerah were silent. They had not expected Pilate to be so difficult.

'Your silence must mean that he has *not* spoken against Rome.' He turned to Quintilius. 'He's a religious crank, Quintilius. I'm glad to have received a report on him, but I've more urgent things to do than deal with this superstitious nonsense.'

Haggai was fast losing his temper, but Zerah laid a warning hand on his arm. 'Your Excellency,' he said, 'the matter is of the utmost importance. The man has been guilty of the most frightful blasphemy, and should suffer the penalty which, under the Law of Moses, blasphemy incurs. This Jesus calls himself the Son of God. Surely Your Excellency can understand – '

'His Excellency,' Quintilius broke in, 'is not interested in your religious riddles.'

'It is not a riddle,' replied Zerah. 'It is a stark affront to the whole nation. The man has defiled our religion. He has affronted God.'

'My only consideration,' retorted Pilate, 'is law and order. Is this man a threat to Roman order?'

'Your Excellency,' said Zerah, 'he has already broken a Roman law.'

'Which law?' demanded Pilate irritably.

'He calls himself the King of the Jews,' Zerah said.

'Has he made the claim explicitly, or is this your interpretation of something he has said about being anointed?' demanded Pilate.

'In the most explicit terms and before many witnesses, Your Excellency, he has claimed to be the King of the Jews,' Zerah assured him. 'And he has told the people not to pay tribute to Caesar.'

'Ah, that would indeed be treason, would it not, Quintilius?'

'It would indeed, Your Excellency,' said Quintilius.

'Very well,' said Pilate. 'I will see what the man has to say for himself. Bring him to me.'

Jesus, who had been standing some way apart surrounded by guards, was now brought forward, and confronted Pilate for the first time.

Pilate looked scornfully at the deputation. 'Is this your dangerous aspirant to kingship?' he asked. 'Tattered, barefoot, emaciated.' He turned and spoke to Jesus. 'The chief priests of your Temple accuse you of leading the people astray.' Jesus remained silent. 'Of telling them not to pay tribute to the Emperor,' continued Pilate. Jesus still gave no answer. 'Of claiming to be the King of Jews,' Pilate persisted. 'Are you the King of the Jews?'

'If my kingdom were of this world, my men would have fought to prevent me being captured.'

'You are a king then?' said Pilate.

'Yes, I am,' said Jesus. 'It was for this that I was born. I came into the world for this: to bear witness to the truth; and all who are on the side of truth listen to my voice.'

'What is truth?' said Pilate, and looked at Jesus in some perplexity. 'Who are you?' he asked.

Jesus looked into the Procurator's eyes. Hardened though Pilate was the steady gaze disturbed him. He looked away to the members of the Sanhedrin. 'I understand neither him nor his words,' he said, 'but I do understand one thing. There are no grounds for condemning him to death.'

His accusers were angered by the judgement, and made no attempt to conceal their feelings. Pilate merely called out to the guards, 'Take him away. Give him a token flogging and then let him go.'

The Roman guards marched Jesus away to a column in a far corner of the courtyard. His garments were torn off in preparation for the flogging, and other soldiers joined the group.

A Roman flogging was a fearful ordeal. It was carried out with a long leathern whip, studded at intervals with pellets of lead and sharpened pieces of bone. Quite literally, it could tear a man's back to ribbons. Men had been known to go mad under the lash, and few retained consciousness to the end.

'Nothing else, is there?' Pilate said to Quintilius as Jesus was led off.

'Well, perhaps Your Excellency should see your orders carried out,' said Quintilius. So Pilate waited, chatting to Quintilius and ignoring the members of the Sanhedrin while Jesus was tied to the pillar and scourged.

Pilate had ordered a token flogging. But the officer in charge was a Syrian, and there were Syrian soldiers among those wielding the lash. As Syrians were great haters of the

Jews, the men naturally put their heart into their work. At last Jesus's head was slack against the column, and the officer called the whipping to a halt. 'Enough,' he said. 'Put his clothes back on.'

'But he said he was a king,' a centurion protested, 'the King of the Jews. Surely we ought to attire him as befits his rank.' He laughed and pulling a purple cloak from the nearest soldier, draped it about Jesus. Another soldier, catching the spirit of the game, disappeared for a moment and returned carrying a branch studded with long piercing thorns. He deftly twisted the branch into the shape of a crown which he placed on Jesus's head and then crushed down. 'Oughtn't he to have a sceptre?' asked the officer, grinning, and a soldier thrust a reed into Jesus's hand.

Advised that the flogging was over, Pilate was about to leave, but the voice of Zerah detained him. While Pilate had studiously ignored them the members of the Sanhedrin had conferred together. Now the voice of Zerah was respectful, but it was strong and insistent. 'Your Excellency,' it said, 'we find it hard to understand why you resist the condemnation of this man. Anyone who claims to be a king is surely speaking treason against Caesar. If you let him go will it not be said that you are no friend of Caesar? And may not a rumour get back to Caesar himself?'

Pilate paused. He was angry, but he was caught in a dilemma. He was satisfied that Jesus was politically harmless, and he had no wish to serve the religious feud of his accusers. But their veiled threats about Caesar were disturbing. His administration had not been too successful, and Caesar was only too ready to listen to damaging rumours. He had been impressed by Jesus but he was certainly not going to take risks for him. Neither was he going to give way to his fanatical accusers without a struggle. So, as though closing the issue, he said, 'It is customary to release a prisoner in celebration of the Passover. I will release this man.'

They reacted with unconcealed anger to this solution of his problem, and he again tried to outwit them. 'The people shall decide,' he said. 'Let the voice of the people be heard.' And he gave orders for the crowd to be admitted to the courtyard. Then he turned to the guards and said, 'Where is he? Bring forth this King of the Jews.'

Jesus was pushed roughly forward, scarce able to stand. Pilate flinched slightly at his appearance. Blood had congealed on his forehead where the crown of thorns had pierced. The purple cloak did little to hide the terrible weals and gashes in his body. Pointing to him, Pilate turned to the crowd which had poured excitedly into the courtyard and said, 'Behold the man!'

To his surprise, for he had expected the Jews to feel sympathy for a Jewish prisoner, the crowd yelled, 'Crucify him!'

'Why, what evil has he done?' Pilate cried.

'He is a false prophet. He said he was equal to God. Crucify him.'

Jesus stood quietly amid the uproar and Pilate was astonished by his dignity. He spoke to him in a low voice. 'Who are you?' he said. 'Why don't you defend yourself? Surely you realize that I have power to crucify or to release you?'

'You would have no power over me,' answered Jesus, 'if it had not been given to you from our Father in heaven.'

Pilate again turned to the crowd. 'It is the Passover,' he said, 'a time of clemency. According to a custom of yours I should release one prisoner. Shall I release this man?'

The Zealots yelled, 'No. Set free Barabbas.' Other voices in the crowd took up the cry. 'Let Barabbas go free. Barabbas. Barabbas. Barabbas.' Amidst the clamour Mary with a few others shouted desperately for Jesus, but their voices were drowned by the shouts for his rival. 'Set Jesus free,' they shouted, 'he is innocent. He is the Messiah. Release Jesus.' But the Zealots shouted still louder. 'Barabbas. Set free Barabbas. Jesus is a false prophet. Crucify him.'

'Barabbas?' Pilate shouted questioningly. The crowd roared still louder. 'Barabbas, Barabbas, Barabbas.' Pilate looked at Jesus. He stood quietly watching the crowd, giving no outward sign of anxiety or despair over his fate.

'Very well,' said Pilate, turning to Quintilius. 'They want Barabbas. They shall have Barabbas. What difference does it make, anyway? I'm sick of the whole business and wish I'd never seen this Jesus. Set Barabbas free.'

'And Jesus?' queried Quintilius.

'I'll sign the death warrant.'

Quintilius was also a bearer of news which he found very distasteful. He appeared in the cell where Barabbas, still shackled, was being held with Aram and Joah, and told the warder to unloose him. Then he motioned towards the open door.

'Now get out,' he said disgustedly to Barabbas.

'The time has come, has it?' said Barabbas. 'Well, do your worst. I spit on Rome and its bloody might. The day of the Lord is coming and then your bloody might will go down in flame and destruction.'

'I could have you re-arrested for that,' said Quintilius, 'but I didn't hear it. Go on. Out. Order for your release. Signed by the Deputy Procurator. As for you two,' he continued, turning to Aram and Joah, 'the order's been signed for your execution.' He turned again to Barabbas who was lingering uncertainly by the warder. 'Why they let you go I'll never understand.'

At this Aram set up his usual protesting whine. 'There must be a terrible mistake', he wailed. 'I'm the innocent one here. I'm the one they meant to release, not Barabbas. I didn't do anything.' Suddenly Joah screamed at Barabbas, 'You sold yourself. That's what you did. You sold yourself to the Roman bastards.' He flung himself at the Zealot but the guards pulled him off.

'Get out before I kick you out,' Quintilius shouted, and the guards dragged Barabbas through the cell door.

Pilate had retired to his own apartments. He looked moodily over the city spread out before him, and picked indifferently at his food. The interruption when Quintilius appeared was welcome.

'The Jews have been back again,' Quintilius told him. 'Dissatisfied as usual. They don't approve of the board stating the Nazarene's crime that's to go up over his cross. It says "Jesus of Nazareth, King of the Jews". They say he only alleged . . .'

'What I have written,' Pilate said harshly, 'I have written.'

As part of the ritual of Roman crucifixion the prisoner was forced to carry the transverse beam of his own cross to the place of execution. Jesus, with the crown of thorns still pressing into his head, was accordingly taken to the fortress woodyard to be saddled with this crushing burden.

As he entered the yard he felt a pang of memory almost more acute than his physical sufferings. The orderly row of tools, the stacks of timber, the chippings littering the floor, the pungent-sweet smell of wood, all carried him back to the carefree days in Joseph's shop when, as a boy, he climbed the ladder and looked out at the roads that stretched to the ends of the earth. Now he was on the road that would end . . .

'That's the lot for today then?' said the carpenter.

'The third and the last,' said the officer. 'You can tie him up.' The cross-beam was lifted and roped to Jesus's lacerated back. In intense pain and weakness he began the walk to Calvary.

The tragic procession had to pass under some arches that opened on to the streets of Jerusalem, close to the fortress. Nicodemus was lurking behind one of the pillars, watching with a bursting heart as Jesus dragged past. Jesus looked at him, and Nicodemus's eyes filled with tears. The recognition caused Jesus to falter for a moment, and a guard pushed him brutally forward. Nicodemus clasped his hands together and broke into uncontrollable weeping. A verse of scripture echoed in his mind: '. . . like a lamb led to the slaughter.'

It was intensely hot. The sun scorched down from a sky that was like a dome of beaten copper. Then the murmur of a sad lament made itself heard. Nicodemus, conscious only of the tragic figure of Jesus, was reciting the prophecy of Isaiah:

'He was despised and rejected of men; a man of sorrows and acquainted with grief, and we hid as it were our faces from him. He was despised and we esteemed him not. Surely he has borne our griefs and carried our sorrows. Yet, we did esteem him, stricken, smitten of God and afflicted. But he was wounded for our transgressions. He was bruised for our iniquities. The chastisement for our sins was laid upon him, and through his wounds we are healed. We all, like sheep, have gone astray, each taking his own way. And the Lord had laid on him the iniquities of us all. He was oppressed and he was afflicted, yet he opened not his mouth. He was brought as a lamb to the slaughter and, as a sheep before its shearer is dumb, so he opens not his mouth.'

The guards, weary of the hostility of the crowd, began systematically prodding Jesus to make him move faster. At last, weak to the point of utter exhaustion, he stumbled and fell. Struggling up he shakily tried to regain his balance, but fell again. A woman emerged from the crowd and mercifully wiped the sweat and blood from his face. His sight cleared for a moment, and he gazed at her face as if to memorize its features. Then he stumbled forward once more.

At last they reached Calvary. Joah had already been fixed to his cross, and Aram, howling and screaming piteously like a wounded animal, was being nailed down. Jesus staggered up the final stretch of the way.

Aram and Joah were now erect on their crosses with a space for the third cross between. As Jesus reached the place of execution some women in dark garments were waiting for him. They were a small group of compassionate ladies who had secured the right to offer drugged wine to the condemned in order to dull the pain when the nails were hammered home. Aram and Joah had gulped down this merciful draught with frantic eagerness. Jesus asked for no stupefying drug, and gently put the cup aside.

There was a disturbance in the crowd. John and Martha, their faces drawn and pale from sleepless anguish, pushed forward to get as near to him as possible. He lay on the ground, as his hands were nailed to the cross-piece to which he was also bound. With professional expertise the soldiers had soon completed their work. Then he was hoisted up and his feet were fastened to the upright. Nicodemus, who had followed with the crowd, was still murmuring to himself. 'God so loved the world that he sent his only begotten son . . .'

Pilate's sign had gone up over the cross, 'Jesus of Nazareth, King of the Jews'. Some Pharisees pressed forward, protesting bitterly. 'It's an insult. Blasphemy. Pull down that inscription. He's not the King of the Jews.' The Roman soldiers ignored them and then, when they grew more importunate, thrust them back into the crowd.

The tortured figures were shifting continuously in a vain effort to ease their pain. Aram, bordering on delirium, screamed wildly at Jesus. 'If you are the Christ why don't you save us?' But Joah, speaking with difficulty, rebuked him. 'Leave him alone. He did nothing wrong. He did – nothing but right.' With a desperate sob he tried to turn his head toward Jesus. 'Remember me when you come into your kingdom,' he said.

'Today,' Jesus said, 'you will be with me in paradise.'

Mary, the mother of Jesus, Martha and Mary of Magdala were trying to make their way through the crowd to the foot of the cross, but those in front were intent on mocking Jesus, and kept pushing them back.

A voice cried, 'If you are what you say you are, why don't you come down from the cross?' Another called, 'He saved others, but can't save himself.' Yet another, 'Show us a miracle. We're all waiting.'

Amid the confused noise of the crowd the jeering voices got through to Jesus. 'Father,' he prayed, 'forgive them, for they know not what they do.'

Mary had reached the front of the crowd and tried to force her way through the cordon of guards. 'I'm his mother,' she pleaded. 'Let me through.'

'How can you prove it?' the sergeant asked.

The centurion whose servant Jesus had healed, shocked by what had happened, but impotent to help, stood dejectedly close by the cross. 'Let these women through,' he said to the sergeant. 'She is his mother.' But when Mary Magdalene came forward he surveyed her uncertainly and asked, 'Who are you?'

'I am one of the family', she said.

He looked at the mother of Jesus and asked, 'Is that right?' She looked at Mary of Magdala, whom she had never seen before. 'Yes,' she said, 'she belongs to us.'

The three women went together to the foot of the cross. The burning sun was vanishing behind a heavy, menacing cloud and the wind was rising strongly. There was a distant mutter of thunder. Some of the simpler people took this weather change as a portent. John and James the Less cautiously appeared. They too pushed their way to the cross. The centurion saw them and they shrank back in fear, but he signed them to come on. 'I remember you,' he said. 'Go to him.'

Jesus looked down from the cross and saw them. 'Woman,' he said to Mary, 'behold your son,' and he looked toward John. Then he said to John, 'Behold your mother.' John put his arm round Mary, and from that moment she became his special care.

The soldiers were still at the foot of the cross. Quartus said, 'Give him something to drink.'

'No,' said Rufo, 'they don't want him to last too long. They've said the Jews can take him down before the Sabbath, because it's the Passover.'

'Never mind about orders,' Quartus said obstinately.

'Pass something up on your spear.'

'Oh, all right, then,' Metellus said. He dipped a sponge in some wine and held it up on his spear. But Jesus turned his head aside and it was taken down again.

'*Eloi. Eloi. Lama sabachthani* . . .' said Jesus. Habakkuk and Haggai, who had gleefully joined in the taunts, overheard him. 'Nailed to a cross even now the blasphemer quotes from a psalm of David,' Habakkuk exclaimed angrily. But just then he became conscious of another voice murmuring at his back. Nicodemus, gazing at Jesus, was continuing the quotation from the psalm. 'My God, my God, why hast thou forsaken me . . . I am poured out like water, and all my bones are out of joint: my heart is like wax . . . the assembly of the wicked have enclosed me: they pierced my hands and feet . . .'

Habakkuk looked uneasily up at the cross. Then he saw the soldiers with their dice. His forehead became beaded with sweat. Was it possible – were the prophecies really being fulfilled?

The voice of Nicodemus still went on, 'They part my garments among them, and cast lots for my clothes . . . But be thou not far from me, O Lord: O my strength, hasten thou to help me.'

Just then Jesus uttered an exclamation of pain. His face, contorted with the pain, became suddenly calm, composed. 'Father,' he said, 'into thy hands I commit my spirit.' His head fell forward. Jesus was dead.

Jesus might be dead but the problem he had created for Caiaphas was by no means at an end. The High Priest had sought audience of Pilate, and had been fortunate to catch the Procurator in the courtyard of the Antonia Fortress, thus avoiding awkward explanations about not entering a heathen dwelling.

'I know how busy you are, my dear Procurator, and shall detain you for only a moment,' he began. 'I have come as a humble suitor with a simple request. At this holy Passover season we cannot have Jewish bodies left hanging on their crosses over the Sabbath. If the men who were crucified are dead, may their corpses be removed?'

'Yes,' Pilate said after reflecting a moment. 'I see no objection. I'll speak to Quintilius about it. He'll give the order. We've certainly had enough of this Jesus of Nazareth, the prophet.'

'A false prophet,' Caiaphas reminded him. 'And it is written in our book of Deuteronomy that "the prophet who presumes in the name of God to say things that God has not commanded, that prophet shall die".'

'Ah. I've not read the book myself,' said Pilate, 'so the force of the reference escapes me.'

Caiaphas ignored the thinly veiled sneer. 'I have a further request, Your Excellency, which concerns this false prophet, Jesus. He said – you may have heard? – that he would rise from the dead.'

'Rise from the dead!' ejaculated Pilate. 'Not after he's had a Roman spear through his heart. Why do you trouble me about such impossible nonsense?'

'I agree, my dear Procurator, that Jesus's claim to rise from the dead is impossible nonsense, as you say. Unfortunately it is the kind of impossible nonsense he dealt in; the stock in trade with which he deceived multitudes. His followers were always telling tales of the marvels and miracles he performed. And it is not at all impossible that they could steal his dead body, hide it away, and give out that he had risen from the dead and was continuing his mission in secret. Issuing orders for the foolish rabble through them.'

'You think that a serious possibility?' said Pilate. 'Well, what is it that you want me to do?'

'Let the man's burial place be guarded for a short time. From what I hear he said he would rise from the dead in three days. Three seems to have been his magical number. He said he would destroy the Temple and rebuild it in three days. A few days' watch – that's all that will be needed. His followers won't dare to approach with Roman soldiers standing by. Then the story will be discredited and his followers finished. The whole sorry business will be at an end.'

Pilate reflected again, and then shrugged. 'It all seems very far-fetched,' he said, 'but I know how rumours grow.' He was about to add 'especially in this fanatical priest-ridden hole' but stopped himself in time. 'Very well,' he said, 'if you insist on guards, guards it shall be. I will give the order.'

Jesus was dead, but Mary his mother, Mary of Magdala, John, James, and Joseph of Arimathea remained in silent vigil at the foot of the cross.

A soldier who had been detailed to break the limbs of the crucified in order to hasten their death, approached the cross. As he did so Quartus called out, 'Don't bother. He's been dead for some time.'

'Orders have been received to get them down quickly,' the man with the iron bar said. 'The show hasn't lasted very long this time.'

'True, but orders are orders. You can give us a hand with the unnailing', Quartus said.

Seeing these preparations for lowering the body, Joseph of Arimathea turned to Mary, the mother of Jesus. 'My family has its own burial place close to Jerusalem,' he said. 'There is a tomb there where we could lay him. It is a strong tomb, carved in rock, not yet used for burial.'

Nicodemus said, 'He should be embalmed as befits his greatness. But the Sabbath will soon be starting. We shall have no time to lose. I will provide bandages and ointment.'

'I have ointment here', whispered Mary of Magdala. 'I used some of it to anoint him when he was alive.'

The storm had declined into a steady dispiriting downpour. His mother looked at his lifeless rainwashed body as the soldiers were removing it from the cross. Up to this point she had controlled herself by a more than human effort, but she now gave vent to a terrible flood of grief. The women gathered round to comfort her, while the men prepared to take up the body and carry it away for burial.

*

It was the morning following the Sabbath. Roman guards were posted round the rock-hewn tomb where the body of Jesus, hastily embalmed on the Friday evening, had been laid to rest. A massive boulder had been pushed into place to seal the tomb's entrance.

Zerah and another Temple official had stationed themselves a short distance apart from the soldiers, and were also keeping watch. Nothing happened the night through, then, with the dawn of Sunday scarcely breaking, they were suddenly alert: Mary Magdalene and the sisters Martha and Mary were walking timidly toward the tomb.

A sentry ordered them to halt. 'Who are you?' he demanded.

'Friends of the man who lies there,' said Mary of Magdala.

'What do you want?'

'To enter the tomb.'

'Is that all?' said the sentry with heavy irony. 'Why do you want to do that?'

'To leave these herbs and spices. It is the custom.'

'Why didn't you do that when they put him in there?'

'Because the Sabbath began,' Mary explained. 'We couldn't buy these things on the Sabbath.'

'Well, perhaps you'll say how you propose to get them in now. It would take a whole squad of men to open that tomb. But you must remain here, I shall have to report you to my officer.' He prodded another soldier who, wrapped in his cloak, was sleeping on the ground. 'Here Lentullus, wake up. You're needed. Message for the officer.'

The light had become a little stronger. Only now did they become aware of two young men working in the garden on a hillock near the path leading to the tomb. One addressed the women cheerfully. 'Why do you seek the living among the dead? Jesus is risen. He is not here.'

The astonished women looked at the tomb. It was already open. The great boulder had been pushed aside. They looked back questioningly at the young man but he was no longer there.

'What's happening?' cried the bewildered sentry. Zerah and the other Temple official hurried forward, realizing with sudden alarm that the tomb was open. Bending down they entered the low doorway.

Everyone was suddenly awake. Lentullus returned with the officer, who began throwing questions at the sentry and the other guards.

He made them repeat their stories many times. 'And that's all you can tell me?' he said angrily at last. 'You were on the alert all night and heard nothing.'

'I can only speak for myself, sir,' the sentry said, 'but I swear by Hercules and Jupiter . . .'

'Yes, yes,' interrupted the officer, 'I've heard all that before. You were wide awake all night long and you didn't budge from the spot.'

'That's right, sir', said the sentry. 'We were given strict instructions. Nobody's been here all night, I swear.'

'Then who moved the stone?' demanded the officer. The men remained silent. 'I don't like this,' said the officer. 'I don't like it at all, there's bound to be trouble. Are you sure you didn't play some sort of game with the thing during the night, just to pass the time?'

'Positive, sir. Those Jewish priests or whatever they are were with us all night. *They* wouldn't play games, sir.'

Zerah emerged from the tomb, panting and angry. 'There is only one explanation', he said. 'His followers came here during the night, they removed the stone.'

'Impossible', said the officer. 'I had officers posted on both sides.'

Zerah shook his head and bending down looked inside the tomb again. There was nothing. 'Now it begins,' he muttered. 'Now it all begins . . .'

As for the disciples, they had gone into hiding. John had relations who were farming not far from Jerusalem, and these sturdy folk had sheltered the disciples in one of their barns. It was a rough place but it was remote, well concealed, and seemed reasonably safe.

Their faces drawn by anxiety and grief, they huddled together round a bench which served as a table, in scarcely broken silence. When someone knocked at the door several of them visibly started. Andrew, who was nearest the door, looked at Peter, to whom they all looked for a lead, and Peter nodded his head. With his hand on the bolt Andrew softly inquired, 'Who's there?'

'Me, Philip,' the voice outside replied. Andrew let him in and promptly shot the bolt again. Without speaking Philip stepped up to the table and turned out the bread and wine from the basket he was carrying.

'Did no one follow you?' asked Bartholomew.

'No. No one.'

'Are you sure?' persisted Bartholomew.

'Of course I'm sure. I took the greatest possible care.'

'Soldiers about?' queried Matthew.

'Yes, everywhere. We must get away from this place.'

'But where can we go?' asked James.

'Back to Galilee. This place is a death-trap.'

'We must keep calm,' said Peter. 'We must think what the Master would have wanted, and do that.'

Thomas shook his head disconsolately. 'The Master is dead,' he said.

Suddenly there was a loud and urgent knocking at the door. They looked round startled, and in a reproachful whisper Matthew said to Philip, 'You told us you weren't followed.'

'I wasn't,' retorted Philip, keeping his voice low.

Again there was a knocking at the door, louder and more insistent. They looked fearfully at one another until Peter, driven by desperation to boldness, went to the door and flung it wide open. 'Why, Mary!' he exclaimed.

Mary of Magdala came into the barn. She seemed in a strange uplifted mood, bursting with excitement yet spiritually serene.

'Peter, Matthew, all of you,' she cried, 'I've seen him!'

'Seen him?' said Matthew. 'Seen who?'

'The Master,' answered Mary. 'I've seen him. So have

Martha and Mary.'

'What on earth are you talking about?' said John.

'He has risen from the dead. He's alive, here.'

'He can't be', said Thomas.

Mary reached for a stool. She was physically tired despite her excitement. 'At the tomb,' she said, 'there was a young man who seemed to be clothed in light. When we asked the soldiers for permission to take herbs and spices into the tomb he said, "Why do you look for the living among the dead? Jesus is not here. He is risen." Then we saw that the stone sealing the entrance had been moved. Martha went in. I saw the grave clothes lying on the ground. We looked for the body, but it wasn't there.'

'The soldiers must have taken it', exclaimed Andrew.

'Let her finish', Peter said.

'When we looked again for the young man', Mary continued, 'he had gone. But then I met another man. I thought he was the gardener. He saw how desperate I was and said, "Why are you weeping?" I said, "Because they have taken the body of my Lord." Then he spoke my name. He said "Mary", and at once I knew. There was no mistaking him when he said that. It was Jesus. I said, "Master." I fell on my knees and clung to him. He said, "Touch me not, for I have not yet ascended to my Father. Go and find the brethren and tell them." And so I came, running much of the way, for I was so excited.'

There was a silence. The disciples looked at each other, wondering and unsure, each waiting for the other to speak first. At last Thomas burst out, 'I can't believe it. I'll never believe it.'

'Do you think I'm mad?' Mary cried. 'I've seen him, I tell you, with my own eyes.'

'Why don't you go home, Mary,' John said sympathetically. 'You're tired. You need a good rest.'

'You'll see him yourself,' Mary cried, vexed almost to tears by their incredulity. 'You'll see him.'

There was an uncomfortable silence. She went to the door.

Andrew let her out, firmly bolting the door again as she slipped away.

'What can you expect,' Thomas said dejectedly. 'An hysterical woman.'

John looked at him thoughtfully. 'You didn't believe when he raised Jairus's daughter,' he said.

'Does that mean you *do* believe her story?' demanded Thomas. He flung the question at the other disciples. 'Do you believe? Can you believe?' No one replied. Then he asked Peter yet again, '*Do* you believe?'

Peter spoke slowly, as though spelling out his thoughts. 'I think I do,' he said. 'After all, it was what he predicted, but we were too frightened by what happened next to take much notice. We all failed him. I failed him worse than any of you. I denied him because I was a coward. But we all deserted him. The members of the Sanhedrin condemned him, but then they didn't know him. We did know him. We ate with him, lived with him, witnessed his mighty acts. We believed he was the Messiah, and still we betrayed him. We are more guilty than those who condemned him. But although we failed him I begin to believe that he won't fail us. He raised others from the dead. Why then should he not triumph over death himself?'

They fell silent, each puzzling over this staggering thought. At last, something made Andrew turn and look towards the barn door. He gasped, making Peter and the others swing round too. They could hardly believe their eyes.

Jesus stood there, silhouetted against the light in the doorway.

Some of the disciples shrank back, more frightened than before, but Peter cried, 'Master!'

'Why are you afraid?' Jesus asked. 'Why do you doubt me? I am here.'

Joy began to dispel the dark shadows from their faces. They were caught up in a great wave of warmth and happiness, as when old friends meet after a long absence. Matthew said, almost laughingly, 'Master, your persecutors will be confused for ever.'

More gravely, but with undiminished affection, Jesus said, 'Why were you so slow to understand? Why were your hearts troubled? Remember the words of the prophets. The Son of Man will suffer and on the third day rise from the dead, and in his name repentance for the forgiveness of sins will be preached to all the nations. Receive the Holy Spirit,' he said. 'Go now like lambs among wolves.'

'Lord,' said Peter, 'stay with us, for the night is falling.'

'Do not fear', said Jesus. 'I will be with you to the end of time. And beyond.'

Principal characters featured in the photographs

Jesus as a man	ROBERT POWELL
Jesus as a boy	LORENZO MONET
Yehuda the Rabbi	CYRIL CUSACK
Herod the Great	PETER USTINOV
Proculus	ROBERT BEATTY
Saturninus	NORMAN BOWLER
Naso	JOHN PHILLIPS
Joseph	YORGO VOYAGIS
Mary	OLIVIA HUSSEY
Elisabeth	MARINA BERTI
Anna	REGINA BIANCHI
Abigail	NANCY NEVISON
The Shepherds:	JONATHAN ADAMS
	ROY HOLDER
	RENATO TERRA
Simeon	RALPH RICHARDSON
The Magi:	
Gaspar	FERNANDO REY
Melchior	DONALD PLEASENCE
Balthazar	JAMES EARL JONES
John the Baptist	MICHAEL YORK
Herod Antipas	CHRISTOPHER PLUMMER
Herodias	VALENTINA CORTESE
Mad boy	KEITH SKINNER
Salome	ISABEL MESTRES
Mary of Magdala	ANNE BANCROFT
Joseph of Arimathea	JAMES MASON
The Adulteress	CLAUDIA CARDINALE
Simon the Pharisee	FRANCIS DE WOLFE

127

The Zealots:

Amos	IAN BANNEN
Joel	OLIVER TOBIAS
Hosias	GEORGE CAMILLER
Saul	OLIVER SMITH
Daniel	ROBERT DAVEY

The Apostles:

Simon Peter	JAMES FARENTINO
Andrew his brother	TONY VOGEL
James the son of Zebedee	JONATHAN MULLER
John his brother	JOHN DUTTINE
Philip	STEVE GARDNER
Bartholomew	JOHN EASTHAM
Thomas	BRUCE LIDINGTON
Matthew the tax-collector	KEITH WASHINGTON
James the son of Alphaeus	SERGIO NICOLAI
Thaddeus	MIMMO CRAO
Simon the Zealot	MURRAY SALEM
Judas Iscariot	IAN MCSHANE

Martha	MARIA CARTA
Zerah	IAN HOLM
Barabbas	STACY KEACH
The centurion	ERNEST BORGNINE
The blind man	RENATO RASCEL
Caiaphas	ANTHONY QUINN
Habbakuk	LEE MONTAGUE
Nicodemus	LAURENCE OLIVIER
Pontius Pilate	ROD STEIGER
Quintillius	TONY LO BIANCO

Director of the TV Film	FRANCO ZEFFIRELLI
Produced by	VINCENZO LABELLA
Executive Producer	BERNARD J. KINGHAM
Associate Producer	DYSON LOVELL
Music composed and conducted by	MAURICE JARRE
Distributed throughout the world by	I. T. C. ENTERTAINMENT LIMITED